A Generation Arising

A Generation after God's Own Heart

The Dawning of a New Day

By

Jocelyn Whitfield

Trilogy Christian Publishers

A Wholly Owned Subsidiary of Trinity Broadcasting Network

2442 Michelle Drive

Tustin, CA 92780

For information, address Trilogy Christian Publishing

Rights Department, 2442 Michelle Drive, Tustin, Ca 92780.

Trilogy Christian Publishing/ TBN and colophon are trademarks of Trinity Broadcasting Network.

For information about special discounts for bulk purchases, please contact Trilogy Christian Publishing.

Manufactured in the United States of America

10 9 8 7 6 5 4 3 2 1

Library of Congress Cataloging-in-Publication Data is available.

ISBN 978-1-64773-955-3

ISBN 978-1-64773-956-0 (ebook)

Contents

A Generation Arising
A Generation after God's Own Heart

Introduction

After tragedy comes victory. In 2018, I wrote *Broken and Divided: America and the Church*. Its primary message was that everything that could be shaken would be. I had no idea in 2018 the extent of the shaking that would take place just two short years later.

Why did God reveal to me that shaking was about to occur? Perhaps it was because the Church had (and still has) left its first love - Jesus. We have failed to make the Great Commission a priority. We devote little attention to living and loving in a way that reflects His kingdom on earth as it is in Heaven.

So here we are...in the midst of shaking-and shaking that continues. Before our eyes, we see everything we have trusted, valued, and believed in shaking and being dismantled. And I do mean EVERYTHING, even the local church. COVID-19, a deadly virus, has shaken the entire world and the idols we have adopted. Moreover, the sad indictment on us, as a body, is that the current state of the Church—those of us who hold ourselves out as followers of Christ—has not been rooted and grounded enough in *Him* to prevent it.

For those reasons, today we are in are in the midst of a reckoning. God has stepped out of eternity, and He has stopped not only the activities of the world, but also all the busyness of the Church. God has loosed His protective hand (though, thankfully, He has not removed it completely), and He has allowed Satan to kill, steal, and destroy for a time. Why? This must be a means to get our attention. We are a world that has lost its way and has turned from God. And, the Church, which is supposed to lead the way to God, too often more closely resembles the world than it does Christ—the One whose image we should bear. While I can't speak for the entire world, I can say that America has become a nation of self-centered profiteers who use communities of faith for political and selfish gains, and the Church is too blinded to see this because we have shunned righteousness and the Lord. The Church has lost its fire. It has gone after its own selfish interests. Leaders have pursued personal agendas and visions, building their kingdoms on earth rather than seeking God's eternal kingdom agenda—the one to which they originally were called.

We turned.

We drifted.

We ignored.

As a result, God, in His love, has permitted shaking to draw us back. Yes, COVID-19 has become a great teacher in this hour...if we are listening.

It is teaching the world a lesson. No matter how powerful, wealthy, or in control we-humans- appear to be, every single one of us is powerless without God.

There is a message for the Church as well. God is not interested in decorating fancy edifices, or erecting more buildings, or increasing congregation size for the sake of boasting. He is interested in one type of construction activity only building the kingdom of God, by saving souls, growing disciples, and making His kingdom visible to the world. God's will is to have a Church to honor Him and to fulfill the Great Commission. His desire is for us to be a people after His own heart – people who will love and obey Him.

Though God has stilled us, *He* remains on the move. God's Spirit is at work stirring, touching, shaping, and transforming hearts. He is raising up, in this very hour, a righteous generation that will love Him and fulfill His kingdom agenda.

That is what the Spirit of the Lord has been sharing with me and urging me to pass on to you:

I am raising up a new generation. Out of the ashes of the past, they are coming forward. For I am doing a new thing, and this will be a new day. I am at work changing their hearts to care about the things that I care about: justice, righteousness, compassion, mercy, and my love for humanity. I am filling them with My Holy Spirit. I am purifying, cleansing, and preparing My called to be a special and holy people unto Me.

I am joining the hearts of My young, as well as the tried-and-true remnant. Together, they will lead the greatest revival and harvest of souls ever known. At that time, I will reveal My glory. The world then will see My unshakeable kingdom. My army is moving forward in power to drive out darkness and evil. I am making them ready, and they are about to be released to make way for the coming of the Lord.

With God's message in mind, I write this book. It is about the generation that God is raising up—a generation after His own heart. It is intended to help you understand the urgency of this time and what the Spirit of Lord is doing, Also, discover who those in the arising generation are, where they are, the mission they have been called to fulfill, and how you can join them and/or be an instrument in furthering God's plan with them. This book is both prophetic and biblical. It is my hope that you grasp the urgency of this moment in time and rise up to become a part of this people after God's own heart—a people wholly committed and devoted to His will.

My Prayer for You

I pray that your spiritual eyes will be opened to see our world as God sees it.

I pray that God will give you understanding and clarity as you read each chapter and word.

I pray that you fully grasp that you were saved not just to enter heaven but that you were called to partner with Christ this very day to achieve the Great Commission and to establish His kingdom on earth.

I pray that you will become a man or woman after God's heart—wholly committed and devoted to Him.

Amen

Chapter 1
The Shaking Continues

Shaking...

It has begun, and it is intensifying. Just look around you. Everything that can be shaken is. Scripture foretold of this moment in time.

So, don't turn a deaf ear to these gracious words. If those who ignored earthly warnings didn't get away with it, what will happen to us if we turn our backs on heavenly warnings? His voice that time shook the Earth to its foundations; this time—[H]e's told us this quite plainly—[H]e'll also rock the heavens: "One last shaking, from top to bottom, stem to stern." The phrase, "one last shaking" means a thorough housecleaning, getting rid of all the historical and religious junk so that the unshakable essentials stand clear and uncluttered.

Do you see what we've got? An unshakable kingdom! And do you see how thankful we must be? Not only thankful, but brimming with worship, deeply reverent before God. For God is not an indifferent bystander. He's actively cleaning house, torching all that needs to burn, and [H]e won't quit until all is cleansed. God [H]imself is Fire! (Hebrews 12:25-29, MSG)

If you've wondered what is going on today, you just read it. This is exactly why the shaking is occurring. God is transforming His Church so it can transform the world. He is cleaning His house— the Church. Judgement first must begin in the house of God. It's judgment time for God's own family. We're first in line. It starts with us. Peter sought to prepare us. "For the time has come for judgement, and it must begin with God's household. And if judgement begins with us, what terrible fate awaits those who have never obeyed God's Good News?" (1 Peter 4:17, NLT)

Transformation, through shaking, has become necessary because we have not been diligent on our own about maintaining a right relationship with God. Second Corinthians 13:5-8 explains it this way: "Test yourselves to make sure you are solid in the faith. Don't drift along taking everything for granted. Give yourselves regular checkups. You need firsthand evidence, not mere ' hearsay, that Jesus Christ is in you. Test it out. If you fail the test, do something about it." We are admonished to be proactive about repentance. However, if the Church will not intentionally take steps to look within and to correct itself, then God will help us do so.

That is just what we are seeing currently. The housecleaning has begun. God is ridding His body of the things that are not of Him - historical and secular junk, man-made traditions, doctrines, ideologies, and religiosities. His desire is for the true Church of Jesus Christ—the Ecclesia—to emerge and for the unshakable kingdom of God to be presented to the world.

He also wants all the world to realize its helpless state and the insufficiency of wealth and human power to sustain it or to save lives from death and disease. With opened eyes, His goal is that more of the unsaved will seek His way. And I hope we are recognizing all of this as we grapple with COVID-19. It has killed thousands worldwide and has affected millions. Presidents and world leaders are moving forward cautiously as the number of those affected by the virus increases daily. Normal activities have been curtailed to prevent further spread of the disease: community has ceased to exist, schools and businesses are closed or have had functions strictly limited, stock markets are at the point of crashing, and good economies now are failing. Doctors are trying their best to understand the disease but are struggling, and scientists have not yet found a vaccine or cure.

Couple that *physical*-health shaking with the *social*-health shaking around us. There is both social and civil unrest spanning the globe, as millions—especially young people—protest against racial injustice and unfair treatment by police toward African Americans. And, with the restrictions on movement that stem from COVID, the whole world has slowed enough to see, in new and often unmistakable ways, the images of unrest and also the recurring unjust activity that has sparked it.

The earth itself also groans. The year 2020 has brought an extremely active hurricane season, floods, wildfires, tornadoes, global warming, and the like. We seem to be affected from all sides. Listen to Jesus's own words about times like these. "It will seem like all hell has broken loose - sun, moon, stars, earth, sea, in an uproar and everyone all over the world in a panic, the wind knocked out of them by the threat of doom, the powers-that-be quaking. And then - then! - they'll see the Son of Man welcomed in grand style - a glorious welcome! When all this starts to happen, up on your feet. Stand tall with your heads high. Help is on the way!" (Luke 21:25-28, MSG).

Jesus's message to His Church is to stand tall because our Help is on the way. So, why does the Church seem so help-*less*? Where is the voice of the Church during these times?

Too many of us are as fearful and in panic as those in the world - fearing death, disease, and loss of finances. Though bombarded with new incidents almost daily, too many Christ followers are in the background, if they are taking any stand, in the fight for liberty and justice for all. Too many are failing to see the connection between the labor pains being experienced in God's creation and the Son's return.

Perhaps we are power-*less* at a time when we should be power-*ful* because of how we have been building. Think about what Jesus taught.

Everyone who hears my teaching and applies it to his life can be compared to a wise man who built his house on an unshakable foundation. When the rains fell and the flood came, with fierce winds bearing upon his house, it stood firm because of its strong foundation.

But everyone who hears my teaching and does not apply it to his life can be compared to a foolish man who built his house on sand. When it rained and rained and the flood came, with wind and waves beating upon his house, it collapsed and was swept away.

Matthew 7:24-27 (TPT)

The Church feels, and certainly seems powerless in this hour to an unbelieving world,. As the Church prays, it wonders if God is listening because it seems as if He is not responding. Even more, the ineffectiveness of our prayers leaves a watching world wondering too—both about the strength of our faith and about the power of the One in whom we claim to believe.

Why does God appear to be silent? Doesn't He see the disaster and how it is negatively affecting His Church and the broader world?

God's silence does mean He is absent or not listening. His silence is purposeful. For, in His silence, just maybe His Church will experience its desire again. Just maybe we'll again become thirsty, long for His presence, and pursue Him, with our whole hearts, to demonstrate our love for Him. Maybe this time of silence will awaken us, and like King David, we will proclaim that, "[a]s the deer pants [longingly] for the water brooks, [s]o my soul pants [longingly] for You, O God. My soul [my life, my inner self] thirsts for God, for the living God." (Psalms 42:1-2, AMP) Just maybe God is silent, waiting for the Church to give Him its heart again. God is giving the Church time to examine itself, make the necessary adjustments, and return to Him—its first love. Although, God appears to be silent, He still is working, cleansing, and purifying His Church. He is rearranging things, repositioning the Church in order to align it with His heart, will, and purpose. He also is giving unbelievers the opportunity to yield to Him, to accept Christ's redemptive sacrifice, and to become His children.

We have an amazing God, who has extravagant love for His Church. He cherishes us so much that He has stepped down from eternity to get us back on the right path. During this season, we have been given time to rearrange our priorities, to put God and His kingdom agenda first, and to become the holy Church upon which His glory will rest. Shaking will continue because the end is near; sin and darkness will continue to cover the earth. However, in the midst of it all, the Church - one after God's own Heart - will arise to usher in the unshakable kingdom of God.

Our Prayer

Father, when you chose David to be king of Israel, You said that You chose him because He was a man after Your own heart, one who would do Your will. Lord, today, we give You our hearts, and we receive Your grace and forgiveness.

We ask for Your cleansing as we examine ourselves. We release our hearts to You, surrender our wills to You, and let go of our selfish desires in favor of Yours. Fill us to overflow with Your Holy Spirit and give us Your heart so it will become ours.

Though it has been unsettling, thank You for being silent in these times, for it has made me long for Your presence. Personally, it has made me see that I had strayed from Your love and from making You my first priority. Lord, I am returning to You. Please renew the intimacy I once had with You. Receive my Love. In Jesus's Name. Amen

Chapter 2

Everything Is Changing: The Birth of a New Generation

There is a time for everything,
and a season for every activity under the heavens:
a time to be born and a time to die,
a time to plant and a time to uproot,
a time to kill and a time to heal,
a time to tear down and a time to build,
a time to weep and a time to laugh,
a time to mourn and a time to dance,
a time to scatter stones and a time to gather them,
a time to embrace and a time to refrain from embracing,
a time to search and a time to give up,
a time to keep and a time to throw away,
a time to tear and a time to mend,
a time to be silent and a time to speak,
a time to love and a time to hate,
a time for war and a time for peace.

(Ecclesiastes 3:1-8, NIV)

There is indeed a time for each and everything, season, and activity under heaven. As we live, we discover that change is inevitable. Children are born. People live, grow old, and die. Seasons change in our lives and in nature.

Change is constant. Interestingly, most of us are quite comfortable with change when it appears to be for our good. On the other hand, let something interfere with the status quo, and we are tempted quickly to revert to the days when things seemed better.

Although change usually causes some level of disruption and inconvenience, this truth is that disruption and inconvenience are not always bad. They actually can work for our good.

Consider COVID-19. This virus has sparked change that most would be hard pressed to see as a benefit in any way, shape, or form. It has been disruptive and deadly. Yet, despite its devastation and darkness, some good actually has resulted.

How could anything so bad also be good?

The good is found in the fact that this virus has prompted us to assess what is of value, what is important, and what should be given priority.

Homes have been positively impacted. Many have recommitted to taking time with family - eating, talking, and praying together. Being shut in for extended periods has tested some marriages but, in the testing, many discovered how far apart they had grown and were prompted to invest in rediscovering intimacy and developing closer relationships to solidify their homes. Young people have been able to bond with their parents in unprecedented ways, uniting around causes for the betterment of our country and seeking God together as a household.

Functioning online, some local churches and ministries also have blossomed, and thousands of people have given their lives to the Lord. Virtual small groups gather, and Bible studies have grown. With the slowed pace, believers are developing a personal relationship with God, maturing in their walk with the Lord, and fellowshipping with other Christ followers in deeper ways outside of the church walls. This period has been a wake-up call for many pastors and clergy, who have examined their hearts, motives, and visions for the churches or ministries they lead. They have been challenged to determine whether they are in line with God's vision for His Church.

So, yes, there is no doubt that COVID-19 has been horrific in so many ways and has brought much change to our daily lives. Yet, we also "know that all things work together for good to those who love God, to those who are the called according to His purpose" (Romans 8:28, NKJV). Our good God "know[s] the thoughts that [He] think[s] toward [us], ...thoughts of peace and not of evil, to give [us] a future and a hope" (Jeremiah 29:11, NKJV). To experience such a peaceful, hope-fulfilling future, though, change must come...in us. Our spiritual lives were changed forever when we received Christ as Savior. We became new creations; our hearts were transformed; and the new journey began—a journey in union with our Father, Lord, and Holy Spirit. For too many of us, though, the growth stopped there, and our passion dimmed after conversion.

But God's pursuit of us has not ceased.

Through the shaking, God is inviting us back to Himself. "Then you will call upon Me and go and pray to Me, and I will listen to you. And you will seek Me and find Me, when you search for Me with all your heart" (Jeremiah 29:12-13, NIV)

God wants us to change so that we can experience more of Him and, as we do so, He can have greater impact on our lives and also through us - His Church - on the larger world. Given how far we have strayed, though, for that to happen, the change in the Church must be radical. He is about to change the structure of the local church and how it operates. He is uprooting doctrines, dogmas, traditions, and agendas - those exercised in the open and those that are hidden - and stripping the Church of its man-made ideologies. He is making leadership changes, shifting authority, and closing some branches down permanently.

A new day is dawning. It is a day focused on Jesus -our soon-coming King. These changes are for the good of the Church and will bring the kingdom agenda to the forefront. As the kingdom agenda is ushered in, the world will see it manifested through His sons and daughters. Not only will we be filled with the Spirit of God, but His leading will be unmistakable in our lives. "For as many as are led by the Spirit of God, these are the sons of God" (Romans 8:14, NKJV).

Even without realizing it, all of creation has been waiting for this time to come. The long, agonizing labor pains that creation has endured soon will end, and delivery of a new generation is about to happen. Creation's pregnant state has been worth it. The kingdom of God is about to be revealed to the world - a righteous generation, wholly committed to God, one after His own heart, full of the Holy Spirit, warriors ready to take territory for the kingdom of God. Creation has been anticipating this generation not only to present Christ in all His glory, but also to be transformers in a world that does not know God or anything about His righteousness

The time of change has come. And, it had to begin with the Church. You know that something major must be in the offing when God Himself steps in.

So, what is next? Christ's church must understand its assignment from God. We have been given the authority to manage the earth and to take dominion. Until we change, become the people God has called us to be, and take hold of our assignment, the world will never change. We are approaching the end times, and we must be busy working to prepare the way of the Lord. Our time in this world, as it currently exists, has been shortened. God is about to wrap up everything. The generation that the world has been waiting for is about to arise, and it will do the extraordinary, letting the world know that the kingdom of God is at hand.

Arise, shine; For your light has come! And the glory of the Lord is risen upon you.

Isaiah, 60:1 (NIV)

Change has come! And, it is a good change...for the Church and for the world.

Our Prayer

Father,

We are the generation for which the world has been waiting. You have called us out - Your Church - as a generation after Your own heart. We are Your offspring, created in Your image, infused with Your Spirit to fill the Earth with Your glory and the knowledge of Christ. We accept Your assignment to manifest Your kingdom here on earth.

Lord, we give You permission to change the trajectory of our lives and to bind our hearts to Yours so that we come to know You more and more and to grasp what is important to You. We accept the empowerment of Your Spirit to demonstrate to the world that we are Your sons and daughters - children in more than name only, but people who truly function as You do.

Please continue Your work in us until Christ be formed and we reflect Him in the world. Give us Your peace and make us steadfast and immovable as we carry the gospel of Jesus Christ to world and do exploits in His Name.

To You be all honor, glory, and power, now and forever, we pray. Amen

Chapter 3

Enters a Generation after God's Own Heart

[W]e will tell the next generation the praiseworthy deeds of the Lord, [H]is power, and the wonders [H]e has done. He decreed statutes for Jacob and established the law in Israel, which [H]e commanded our ancestors to teach their children, so the next generation would know them, even the children yet to be born, and they in turn would tell their children.

Psalms 78:4-6 (NIV)

God told Abraham, "I'm establishing [M]y covenant between [M]e and you, a covenant that includes your descendants, a covenant that goes on and on and on, a covenant that commits [M]e to be your God and the God of your descendants" (Genesis 17:7, MSG).

As you can see, generations are important to God. It is His intent that the relationship between Him and His people continues. God's connection to humankind is not to rest with one generation and then stop; rather, it is to be passed on from generation to generation and so on.

Just as God's relationship with His children is to flow from generation to generation, so are the assignments He has for us. When one generation transitions, [H]e has the next being prepared to take its place. In recent times, many of our spiritual giants have gone home to be with the Lord, and many are wondering who will take their places. It just may be that God will not call a human being to lead His people as we near the end times. Instead, I believe that it may be the Holy of Spirit of God Himself who will lead His people.

Under the leadership of the Holy Spirit, God is calling a generation forward to advance His mission. God's message to us is this:

I am raising up a generation that will not be bound by four walls, religious traditions, ideologies, or the doctrines of men. For I am raising up those who will give Me their full attention, who will seek to know My heart, and who will be wholeheartedly devoted to Me.

Upon these will My Spirit rest. They will know My Voice when I speak. They will hunger to know what is important to Me. Their desire will be to obey Me—go right when I say go right and change when I say change. I am raising up a generation that has forsaken their personal agendas and that takes great pleasure in advancing with My kingdom agenda. My Spirit will lead them, and they will follow. I will show Myself strong in them, and they will know me.

I am raising up a generation whose hearts are like Mine and who will give their hearts completely to Me. Think back to David, the son of Jesse. I viewed him as a man after My own heart—one who would do My will—and, because of that, I anointed him king of Israel after I chose to remove King Saul because of disobedience (Acts 13:21-22). So today, I am raising up a generation after My own heart to do My will. Like Samuel did with David, My Holy Spirit is picking them out from the crowd, and I am preparing, equipping, and training this generation to be My army.

Why is the emergence of a generation after God's own heart so important now?

Each day the world gets darker as unrighteousness prevails. To counter the darkness, God wants His light to shine brightly in and through His people. When Israel was coming out of exile, God sent this message of hope to them through the Prophet Isaiah:

Arise, shine; for your light has come,
and the glory of the Lord rises upon you.
See, darkness will cover the earth
and thick darkness is over the peoples,

but the Lord rises upon you
and [H]is glory appears over you.
Nations will come to your light,
and kings to the brightness of your dawn.
Lift up your eyes and look about you:
All assemble and come to you;
your sons come from afar,
and your daughters are carried on the hip.
Then you will look and be radiant,
your heart will throb and swell with joy;
the wealth of the seas will be brought to you,
to you the riches of the nations will come.

Isaiah 60:1-5 (NIV)

We are about to see change. God is preparing to raise up His elect- a multigenerational group of His choosing, made up of young people and His holy remnant.

Take a look around you, and you might begin to recognize them. They are rising up among you. Joining a holy group of trusted, long-time soldiers is an emerging team. They are young people, as well as some who are slightly older but new in the faith- people from every nation, race, and ethnic group, seeking God's presence, worshipping Him unashamedly, anointed by the Spirit of God, and bringing His presence wherever they go. They are radical and bold warriors, coming from every walk of life, every neighborhood, every background - all ambassadors who have had a life-changing encounter with God.

Also, being tapped by the Spirit are young ministers, who have accepted God's challenge both to preach the gospel and to care for the least of these and, in so doing, they serve as the heart, hands, and feet of Jesus. They often don't resemble their more-established colleagues in appearance, speech, or action, nor is their mission field limited to church pulpits. Instead, like Jesus, they minister everywhere. The world is their platform. They are found in bars, concerts halls, on the streets, and elsewhere proclaiming the gospel and ministering to basic human needs of people. They even may be found protesting for justice and righteousness. They are warriors and worshippers, and they go where the Spirit of our God leads.

God can, and will, use this new generation to shine the light so the whole world can see. He even will begin to work through those who are not yet believers. The prophecy of Joel declares that God's Spirit would fall upon *all* flesh, not only on the sons and daughters of believers, but on *all* flesh, every kind of people. And, when that occurs, our sons and daughters will prophesy (Joel 2:28, NIV).

If God's word is to be trusted (and we know that it is), in the next season we will see a massive host of young people on fire for God, proclaiming the power of the gospel to the lost. They will pierce darkness with the arrow of the Holy Spirit, and many of the unsaved - especially the young - will enlist in God's army. I know you might think that I have lost my mind. But I have heard from God; so just watch and see. I feel the atmosphere changing; the Holy Spirit is moving and resting upon our young people. They, walking the power of Holy Spirit, will be the world changers that we have been waiting for. In those who are called, there will not be a desire for fame or for their flesh to be glorified. They only will be interested in living in way that brings glory and honor to God.

Let me offer, as an example, the Black Lives Matter movement. Go with me for a moment. I truly believe God is using that effort for His purposes. Let me explain.

We are seeing young people from across the globe, joining together in unity to protest against racial injustice and inequity. Despite health concerns related to the pandemic, they risk their lives to take a stand and to declare that the way America is treating its citizens of color -especially those who are black and brown - must be addressed through changes in law, policy, and daily practice. Though the group's Marxist leadership may try to own it, they have no idea that they are involved in a move of the Spirit.

Only the Spirit of God could have corralled so many worldwide to take up the cause of racial justice and righteousness. Group leaders may be the ones highlighting these inequities before the cameras, but don't be fooled; God is the middle of it, and *He* will complete it.

You may ask why God would use a Marxist group to carry the banner against racial injustice. God will use whomever He chooses to do His will. If the Church will not stand up for justice and righteous, He will raise up someone else who will do so - even a foe of His people. Think back to the time when the Israelites veered from God's path, and His anger was kindled against them. What did He do? He used an enemy nation to chastise them for their disobedience and for falling into idolatry. In Judges chapter 3, the Bible tells us that "[t]he children of Israel again did evil in the sight of the Lord. So, the Lord strengthened Eglon, the king of Moab, against Israel, because they had done evil in the sight of the Lord" (v. 12, NIV). It is not unheard of for God to use those who are His children's enemies to drive the message home to them that they need to change. It happened then. Is it impossible for God once again to send His message through an unexpected spokesperson of the need for repentance - this time to address more than 400 years of unfair treatment, rape, murder, and more, while the Church too often remained silent and refused to stand up righteousness?

Again, this movement is not Christ-focused, and it certainly has not been perfect. However, even the issues and the disruptors will not stop God's justice. What they have meant for evil, God will turn around for good (Genesis 50:20). God wants justice - oceans of it. He wants fairness - rivers of it (Amos 5:24). Our God loves righteousness and justice and, ultimately, He will see it prevail (Psalm 33:5).

God's choice for an emerging generation may not come in a neat, pretty church package; they may not be dressed in cute dresses or in suit and ties. In fact, they might be more like John the Baptist with the spirit of Elijah than like meek lambs in their Sunday-go-to-meetin' best. Regardless of how they appear on the outside, though, look closely for God's chosen - those who love Him dearly and will not compromise their holiness for comfort or status. They are full of the Holy Spirit, and they follow His guidance to move in power and authority. Some are new converts while others are returning to their first love.

Though many, they march as one. They are the army of the Lord. This is God's new breed. Their assignment is to proclaim the kingdom message to the world and to share the gospel in order to introduce the world to the only One who can deliver those in bondage to the devil. God intends for Christ's light, shining through them, to overtake darkness. The Spirit of the Lord is equipping, training, and releasing them into the world for His glory. They are being prepared to make straight the pathway of the Lord. God's army is rising, and He will be victorious!

Our Prayer

Father,

Start with me. Please do what you need to do in my life to make me a part of Your army. Shape my heart, my mind, and every part of me to be wholly and completely Yours.

Next, I join with my brothers and sisters in Christ. As Your chosen ones for this time, we commit our lives to You. We are humbled that we get to participate in your destiny for the world. You have given us authority and have empowered us with the Holy Spirit to do the work that is necessary to transform our world by introducing others to Christ. We are the generation that You have chosen to usher in the greatest harvest the world has ever seen. We thank You for choosing us. Let us be filled with the Holy Spirit. Keep us in Your love so that the world will know You through us. Prepare us, equip us, and then mobilize us to do You work of the kingdom.

In Jesus's name, we pray, Amen

Chapter 4
The Army of the Lord Is Arising

Stand up! Stand up for Jesus! Ye soldiers of the cross!
Lift high His royal banner; It must not suffer loss:
From victory unto victory, His army shall He lead,
Till every foe is vanquished, And Christ is Lord indeed.

There is a war still going on between darkness and light. It is the battle for souls, even ours, as we near the coming of our Lord. Every day we are in a battle for our lives and the lives of others.

In fact, the battle actually has intensified because Satan senses that his time is short. It's about to wrap up; Jesus is on His way back. Satan's evil forces and his massive team of imps have been released and given the orders to kill, steal, and destroy. The purpose for this mission is to prevent the Church from achieving Christ's Great Commission - "to go and make disciples of all nations, baptizing them in the name of the Father and of the Son and of the Holy Spirit, and teaching them to obey everything [Christ has] commanded" (Matthew 28:19 - 20, NIV).

It appears that Satan has been successful at doing his job...for now. Nations are in shambles. Apostasy is growing, and people are embracing many small "g" gods. There is war, destruction, and death all around us. Real peace seems out of reach.

Even the body of Christ does not seem immune from the enemy's attack. However, Church leaders have been so preoccupied with status and trappings that they seem to have forgotten that they are at war and have been given a precious assignment from their Commander-in-Chief - God Himself. Because of their lack of attention, the Church is ill-equipped to thwart the enemy's attacks. Honestly, most Christ-followers are ignorant of the fact that they are even in spiritual warfare. Many Christians actually may not be under attack because they are such weak threats that attacking them is pointless. And those who are slightly stronger often see their conflicts as being with other humans rather than being a skirmish with the true source. However, we are told in Ephesians 6:12 (NKJV) that "we do not wrestle against flesh and blood, but against principalities, against powers, against the rulers of the darkness of this age, against spiritual hosts of wickedness in the heavenly places."

Ignorance may feel like bliss, but it can destroy us. Lack of awareness often leaves God's own children vulnerable to the tactics and the devices Satan uses to upend them. The result is that many, who should be victorious, live defeated and powerless lives because they have no knowledge of the warfare going on, much less of the effective weapons of engagement given to us by God Himself.

Though the Church has been impaired, wounding is not enough. As we move near the end times, attacks will be intensified. The intent is to annihilate the Church, and any who may be likely to join its ranks, so that the powers of darkness can prevail. Satan's mission is to prevent the world from taking hold of the glorious gospel of Jesus Christ, which will bring them eternal life with God and peace.

Do not be fooled. The enemy is crafty and tailors his schemes to attack us where we are most vulnerable. Don't be swayed to think that you are safe just because you don't hold an official church position. If you follow Christ, you represent the kingdom of God and, for that reason, the devil hates you and is devising plans to defeat you.

How does he fight? His major strategy is deception. He uses manipulation, seduction, counterfeiting, partial truth, and complete lies in the areas of our lives where we are at the greatest risk. He is subtle, sneaky, and undermining. He camouflages himself as an angel of light and seeks to lure us into worshipping him and by enticing us with false means of meeting legitimate needs - perhaps food, clothing, or relationships - that get twisted into idols. He is the perpetuator of all evil and is behind every act of violence and all confusion.

He battles in the world, and he strategically works undercover in the life of the Church. It is not uncommon to recognize Satan posing as an agent of Christ, sometimes even in the pulpit teaching a watered-down, confused, or inaccurate version of the gospel of Christ. It is his spirit at work that seeks to steal the word of God from the hearts of men and women by bringing doubt, conflict, and other problems into our lives - sometimes even before the last "Amen" of the church service is uttered- in order to weaken our faith and power.

Please note that none of this is a surprise to God. Our omniscient Jesus knew the devil's mission and his methods. That is why He gave us His authority to destroy the works of the enemy, and He provided weapons for our use in spiritual warfare. As not only the body of Christ, but also the army of Christ, God sent His Holy Spirit to us to prepare and equip us for the battle He knows we are enmeshed in daily.

In this hour as never before, the Holy Spirit is moving upon the Church - the soldiers of the cross - to equip us for spiritual warfare. God is raising up a righteous generation of warriors - a massive and fierce army - to rise up, to push back, and to debilitate the kingdom of darkness and manifest His Kingdom of righteousness in the Earth.

Think about military forces here on earth. No soldier enters warfare without being sufficiently trained and equipped for the job at hand. An ill-equipped soldier will surely be injured, perhaps killed, and likely defeated. To lessen those chances, soldiers train. They receive rigorous bootcamp training to ready them for combat. They are required to learn basic combat skills and tactics. They become masters of weaponry. They submit to strenuous physical and mental preparation to build their confidence, character, and endurance. And their skills are tested and honed on a continual basis.

Why should we expect anything less of God?

If training is required to serve in a human army, then surely a soldier in God's army must undergo basic training as well. Such preparation for spiritual warfare is needed to equip all believers for the spiritual battles they will encounter in this war between righteousness and unrighteousness, between darkness and light.

Jesus knew the spirit of anti-Christ would come and that His followers would be persecuted. In fact, Jesus told His disciples they would have trouble in this but to take heart that He had overcome the world (John 16:33). Not only did He warn them of impending trouble, Jesus also readied them. For three years, He equipped them with the tools that they could use to combat the attacks of enemy and to deliver those oppressed and in bondage. Jesus's instruction wasn't delivered in a formal classroom. Instead, as Jesus traveled with His disciples, He modeled and explained how to heal the sick, cast out demons, and raise the dead. He gave them authority, in His name, to destroy the works of the enemy and to set people free from Satan's control. He also provided opportunity for them to apply what they were learning while He still was physically with them. Scripture records one such experience.

[T]he Master selected seventy and sent them ahead of [H]im in pairs to every town and place where [H]e intended to go. ***

The seventy came back triumphant. "Master, even the demons danced to your tune!"

Jesus said, "I know. I saw Satan fall, a bolt of lightning out of the sky. See what I've given you? Safe passage as you walk on snakes and scorpions, and protection from every assault of the enemy. No one can put a hand on you.

Luke 10:1, 17-19 (MSG)

Christ give His followers authority over the enemy, and the Apostle Paul taught the Church about weapons that it has at its disposal to successfully destroy the works of the devil. In Ephesians, Chapter 6, he writes:

Now my beloved ones, I have saved these most important truths for last: Be supernaturally infused with strength through your life-union with the Lord Jesus. Stand victorious with the force of [H]is explosive power flowing in and through you.

Put on God's complete set of armor provided for us, so that you will be protected as you fight against the evil strategies of the accuser! Your hand-to-hand combat is not with human beings, but with the highest principalities and authorities operating in rebellion under the heavenly realms. For they are a powerful class of demon-gods and evil spirits that hold this dark world in bondage. Because of this, you must wear all the armor that God provides so you're protected as you confront the slanderer, for you are destined for all things and will rise victorious.

Put on truth as a belt to strengthen you to stand in triumph. Put on holiness as the protective armor that covers your heart. Stand on your feet alert, then you'll always be ready to share the blessings of peace.

In every battle, take faith as your wrap-around shield, for it is able to extinguish the blazing arrows coming at you from the [e]vil [o]ne! Embrace the power of salvation's full deliverance, like a helmet to protect your thoughts from lies. And take the mighty razor-sharp Spirit-sword, of the spoken Word of God.

Ephesians 6:10-18 (TPT)

Although every piece of the armor plays a vital role in battle, I want to highlight one Ephesians 6 weapon in particular - the word of God - and share three others that I believe are equally as important in the fight - prayer, praise and worship, and the person of the Holy Spirit.

The Word of God, the Sword of Spirit

As a soldier of the Lord's army, it is critically important to know the mind of our Captain Jesus. Afterall, He is God. He was there in the beginning of creation. He was the spoken word of God in creation. He is the word become flesh - the Jesus who brought us the gift of salvation and who dwelt among the disciples teaching them the ways of the Father.

Not only is Jesus the word of God, He used the word as His own tool in battle. He reminded Satan of God's word when Satan tempted Him in the wilderness. Satan came to him three recorded times trying to seduce Him into following him rather than God. Each time, Jesus's rebuttal was the word of God (Luke 4:1 - 13).

That tremendous tool - the Word of God - has been given to the Church as both an offensive and defensive weapon to be used in warfare. God's word is the only thing that has the power to destroy the works of the enemy. It is sharper than a two-edged sword (Hebrews 4:12).

The word of God is the one piece of armor that cannot be dismantled or destroyed. It comes from God the Father, represents Jesus the Son, and is inspired by the Holy Spirit. When it is spoken, it puts the forces of devil on the defensive. Nothing and no one are impervious to God's word.

No matter how powerful the Word of God is, though, if we are unaware that we have this weapon or if we are unskilled in using it, we will suffer defeat in spiritual warfare. Fighting the forces of hell without this vital piece of armor, or with armor that we can't handle, leaves us defenseless from the attacks of the enemy. Remember the story of young David when he volunteered to stand up to Goliath, who was taunting the Israelite army.

Then Saul outfitted David as a soldier in armor. He put his bronze helmet on his head and belted his sword on him over the armor. David tried to walk but he could hardly budge.

David told Saul, "I can't even move with all this stuff on me. I'm not used to this." And he took it all off.

Then David took his shepherd's staff, selected five smooth stones from the brook, and put them in the pocket of his shepherd's pack, and with his sling in his hand approached Goliath.

***

David answered, "You come at me with sword and spear and battle-ax. I come at you in the name of God-of-the-Angel-Armies, the God of Israel's troops, whom you curse and mock. This very day God is handing you over to me. *** *And everyone gathered here will learn that God doesn't save by means of sword or spear. The battle belongs to God - [H]e's handing you to us on a platter.*

1 Samuel 17:38-40, 45-47 (MSG)

Why is this story significant? David couldn't use unfamiliar battle tools. Success came only when David picked up what he knew. He knew his slingshot, and he knew God and His word. Yes, David formally killed Goliath with a stone and sling, but he knew that this favorable outcome was not based on his ability alone but his confidence in the power, knowledge and the Name of the Lord. This battle was the Lord's and that, because it was God's fight, he could not be defeated.

The Word of God can be used both offensively and defensively. However, as believers, we must not only hear God's word and its truth, but we must also be prepared to speak it as well. When the word of God is spoken, it becomes an unparalleled weapon in warfare. All of heaven backs us up. The angelic host rallies. The power of God is released as a lethal weapon to stop the attacks of the enemy. Further, as an offensive weapon, God's work can be used to destroy the works of the enemy. Whether wielded on defense or on offense, the Word will not return void but will accomplish what God intended to achieve with its use (Isaiah 55:11, NIV. God's word has dynamite power when released out of our mouths in faith.

Prayer

Interestingly, in Paul's eyes, prayer was a natural partner to the pieces of armor that Christians must be skilled at using in spiritual warfare. As he instructed, "[i]n the same way [as the armor], prayer is essential in this ongoing warfare. Pray hard and long. Pray for your brothers and sisters. Keep your eyes open. Keep each other's spirits up so that no one falls behind or drops out" (Ephesians 6:18, MSG).

The importance of prayer cannot be overstated in battle. We are to "pray without ceasing" (1 Thessalonians 5:17, NKJV). Peter Wagner says that prayer is powerful enough to move God's hand in order to determine the destiny of a whole nation. It is the glue that keeps us in relationship with our Father because it is one of the ways we communicate with Him. When we pray, our ears are opened to hear the voice of God and to receive encouragement, instruction, direction, and peace. Through prayer, we gain access to His power and strength for every battle we face.

Have you ever wondered why it sometimes seems difficult to find time to pray? Do you find that things just seem to get in the way of spending time to communicate with God? Well, this isn't happenstance; it actually is a strategy of Satan to keep you distracted and to disrupt your connection with God. He cleverly presents distractions - busyness, family issues, financial challenges, noisy neighbors, ringing phones, obsession with sports, etc. These are but a few of the interruptions, or even the idols, that steal time from our prayer time with God. Prayer is the mechanism God has given us to us to invite Him into the issues of our daily activities. And, if Satan can keep us from connecting with our power source, we become vulnerable in the fight.

As we look at the lives of Old Testament kings and prophets as well as at New Testament apostles, we see that they were all people of prayer. In fact, prayer typically was the first action step taken when direction was needed to solve problems or when it was time for battle.

For instance, when Nehemiah heard that the walls of Jerusalem were demolished by the Babylonians, he became very distressed about the destruction and the plight of God's people. What was his first action? He sought God in prayer and fasting, crying out for many days in repentance for mercy and help (Nehemiah 1:4). By inviting God into this dire situation, when the king saw Nehemiah's sadness, it opened the door to a discussion that not only gave Nehemiah permission to travel and oversee the rebuilding Jerusalem's walls but that also moved the king to finance the project.

As always, Jesus is our best example. Jesus was a man of prayer. Throughout the gospels, there are records of Him modeling the importance of taking time to speak to, and hear from, the Father. (See, e.g., Matthew 14:23 and 26:36; Mark 6:46 and 13:33; Luke 6:12 and 9:28; and John 14:16.) Jesus prayed in the morning and at night. He prayed before He raised Lazarus from the dead (John 11:41-42). Before His ascension He prayed for Himself, for His disciples, and for all of us who would come after them (John 17).

Not only did Jesus provide an example of how someone incorporates prayer into daily life, He also gave His disciples a pattern of prayer to follow. In other words, He taught His disciples how to pray.

Whenever you pray, be sincere and not like the pretenders who love the attention they receive while praying before others in the meetings and on street corners. Believe [M]e, they've already received in full their reward. But whenever you pray, go into your innermost chamber and be alone with Father God, praying to [H]im in secret. And your Father, who sees all you do, will reward you openly. When you pray, there is no need to repeat empty phrases, praying like those who don't know God, for they expect God to hear them because of their many words. There is no need to imitate them, since your Father already knows what you need before you ask [H]im. Pray like this:

"Our Father, dwelling in the heavenly realms,
may the glory of [Y]our name

be the center on which our lives turn.
Manifest [Y]our kingdom realm,
and cause [Y]our every purpose to be fulfilled on earth,
just as it is fulfilled in heaven.
We acknowledge [Y]ou as our Provider
of all we need each day.
Forgive us the wrongs we have done as we ourselves
release forgiveness to those who have wronged us.
Rescue us every time we face tribulation
and set us free from evil.
For [Y]ou are the King who rules
with power and glory forever. Amen"

Matthew 6:5-13 (TPT)

Prayer glorifies God and reinforces our need for Him. It is interesting that Paul concluded his list of spiritual armor with this reminder, along with truth, righteousness, peace, faith, salvation, and the word of God as the sword, that prayer is just as essential. Clearly, if we are to be successful in spiritual warfare, we need the power of God.

Praise and Worship

An examination of the mighty weapons in spiritual warfare would be incomplete without mentioning the importance of praise and worship as strategic weapons.

First, what are these two parts of the Church's arsenal?

Praise is lifting God up. It is acknowledging His importance in our lives. And, as we see throughout Scripture, praise often is spoken. "I will declare Your name to my brethren; In the midst of the assembly, I will sing praise to You" (Hebrews 2:12, NKJV).

Praise can be a part of worship, but *worship* involves showing reverence to God. When we worship, we lower ourselves in humility before our Creator. Revelation 19:4 describes a scene of worship as, "the twenty-four elders and the four living creatures fell down and worshipped God who sat on the throne, saying Amen! Alleluia!"

Praise and worship have enormous power. They usher God's presence onto the scene. In openly recognizing who He is and humbling ourselves to Him, we invite God in, and He becomes involved in our battle by fighting with and for us.

The Bible affirms the importance of praise and worship in battle. It was customary for kings and warriors to build altars and worship God before going to war. For instance, in 2 Chronicles, we see that Judah was about to be attacked by the Moabite, Ammonite, and neighboring armies, King Jehoshaphat was afraid, but turned immediately to God, seeking wisdom and direction. He gathered the people, proclaimed a fast, and reached out to God through praise and worship (2 Chronicles 20:1-4).

He first acknowledged who God is, "Lord, the God of our ancestors, are [Y]ou not the God who is in heaven? You rule over all kingdoms and nations. Power and might are in [Y]our hand, and no one can withstand [Y]ou (2 Chronicles 20:6, NIV).

Jehoshaphat's prayer also included worship by recognizing his and the nation's standing to God, how helpless they would be without His intervention. "[N]ow here are men from Ammon, Moab and Mount Seir[.]*** For we have no power to face this vase army that is attacking us. We do not know what to do, but our eyes are on [Y]ou" (v.10,12).

In response to Jehoshaphat prayer of praise and worship, God responded:

Listen, King Jehoshaphat and all who live in Judah and Jerusalem! This is what the Lord says to you: "Do not be afraid or discouraged because of this vast army. For the battle is not yours, but God's. Tomorrow march down against them. *** You will not need to fight in this battle. Take up your positions; stand firm and see the deliverance the Lord will give you, Judah and Jerusalem. Do not be afraid; do not be discouraged. Go out to face them tomorrow, and the Lord will be with you. (vv. 15-17)

That next morning, Jehoshaphat chose men to sing to God and praise Him as they went off to the fight. "Give thanks to the Lord, for [H]is love endures forever" (v. 21). The Bible tells us that, "[a]s they began to sing and to praise, the Lord set ambushes against the men of Ammon and Moab and Mount Seir who were invading Judah, and they were defeated" (v.22).

God has not changed. He still inhabits the praises of His people (Psalms 22:3).

When we praise and worship God during battle, we can be assured He will respond. He will come alongside us, sometimes even fighting the battle for us completely as He did for Israel in the 2 Chronicles story, or other times providing the strategies we are to use to defeat the enemy as He did for Israel in the taking of Jericho (Joshua 6).

Because they are such powerful tools, we should also be mindful. Satan will erect any barrier possible and use every available tactic to keep us from praising and worshipping God. Satan does not want us to worship God because he desires to be worshipped. It was his desire to have God's position, power, seat, glory, and standing that got him thrown out of heaven (Isaiah 14:12-21). And today he still is competing for the worship and honor that only God deserves.

Whether we worship God in song, or lay prostrate, or speak with our voices, or use the way we live, it is important to recognize that the praise and worship of God aids us in the fight. Praise and worship, through any means, glorifies God and ushers in His presence to bring salvation, healing, and deliverance to lives that are in bondage to sin.

They dispel darkness. When we choose to praise and worship Him, especially in the midst of war, the enemy becomes confused, and with confusion comes powerlessness and impotence because praise and worship brings God's presence on the scene.

Evil cannot coexist in God's presence. So, pick up praise and worship as effective and strategic weapons as you engage in spiritual warfare.

Your Greatest Weapon Against the Enemy:
The Captain of the Army, The Holy Spirit

The greatest spiritual weapon of all in the arsenal is the person of the Holy Spirit. Every soldier in God's army has access to the Holy Spirit's power. His Spirit lives within each believer and, besides guiding us through normal events, He is ready to be accessed in times of conflict.

Throughout the Bible, we discover the Holy Spirit's presence in action. We see His presence in creation. Genesis 1:2 tells us that "the Spirit of God was hovering over the face of the waters." He was present in the lives of judges and prophets, as His Spirit came upon them, and they prophesied and performed miracles. We read in Judges 3:10 (NKJV) that "[t]he Spirit of the Lord came upon [Othniel], and he judged Israel." Scripture relates how Samuel shared God's word with Saul, advising him that "the Spirit of the Lord will come upon you, and you will prophesy...and be turned into another man" (1 Samuel 10:6, NKJV). We learn that the Spirit descended as a dove upon Jesus as He began His ministry (Matthew 3:16). Moreover, Acts Chapter 2 shares how the early Church was filled with the Holy Spirit, who empowered them to do the mighty works of God.

The Spirit of the Living God isn't simply a part of the Church's past, however. Today, He still is our power source, teacher, helper, advocate, guardian, and guide. God has given us Himself, through the person of Holy Spirit, so we can be assured victory in every battle we face, if we ask for His help.

The Holy Spirit lives in us, and we know that greater He who lives in us than anyone or anything in this world (1 John 4:4). How can we say that? Scripture teaches us that God is omniscient and omnipresent; that is, He knows all and is everywhere (Proverbs 15:3; Psalms 139:1-18; Ephesians 1:9-11). Because of these attributes, God clearly knows every intent, strategy, and action of the devil. Revelation 19:6 also tells us that God is omnipotent. He is more than able to act quickly on our behalf while at war and to give us instructions to advert the attacks of the enemy, show us things to come, provide wisdom, and fortify us in preparation for every spiritual attack that comes our way.

If we follow the directives of the Holy Spirit, He will fight for us (Exodus 14:13-14; Nehemiah 4:20). He will enable us to take territory from the enemy, overcome the forces that would come against us, and set the captives free.

The Army of the Lord is rising!

Let me pause before closing out this chapter. It is one thing to know about God's army and His charge, but it is something entirely different to be an enlisted soldier. So, please, take a few moments now - just you and God - and honestly assess where you stand.

- Are you really a member of God's army?
- Are you willing to engage in the warfare necessary to bring God's kingdom to this world?
- Are you equipped with, and able to use, the spiritual weapons God has given us to become effective soldier in his army?

Whatever your answers, it's never too late to partner with God in this fight. And, if you already are a solider, it's never too late to commit to becoming stronger and more dedicated each day. Are you in?

The Soldier's Prayer

Teach us, Father, how to endure hardship as a good soldier of Jesus Christ. Help us not to be so overwhelmed by the cares of life that either we forget that we are soldiers in your army, or we become distracted and ineffective in battle. No one engaged in warfare entangles himself with the affairs of this life, that he may please Him who enlisted Him as a soldier.

Help us to remember that spiritual warfare cannot be fought in the flesh; instead, battles against demon forces, principalities, and powers in high places require a different approach—Your approach. Help us to be prepared daily to pick up the warfare weapons You have supplied. Help us never forget that this war cannot be won in our own strength, but that victory lies only in the Holy Spirit's power to dismantle strongholds and destroy the work of the enemy.

Thank You for giving us Your armor to subdue the enemy - the belt of truth, the breastplate of righteousness, the gospel of peace, the shield of faith, the helmet of salvation, the sword of Spirit - all of which are aspects of our Savior and Lord, Jesus Christ! In whose mighty name, we pray, Amen

Chapter 5

Intergenerational Transfer-Mentoring the Arising Generation

And don't be intimidated by those who are older than you; simply be the example they need to see by being faithful and true in all that you do. Speak the truth and live a life of purity and authentic love as you remain strong in your faith.

So, until I come, be diligent in devouring the [w]ord of God, be faithful in prayer, and in teaching the believers.

1 Timothy 4:12-13 (TPT)

Intergenerational transfers have been occurring since the beginning of time. It is not uncommon for one generation to teach and pass down essential information - culture, history, and faith - to the next.

The transfer often occurs through storytelling. Parents, grandparents, aunts, uncles, or other elders draw a younger person near to share lessons learned, to impart wisdom, or to relay family history. While in some respects this is just normal family life, in more formal settings this may occur through a mentoring relationship.

Whatever the scenario, it is the responsibility of every generation to acquaint the next generation with the mighty work charged to us by God and to build a bridge so that those that follow are able to continue the work of the Lord. Scripture tells us that one generation shall praise the works of Lord to another and declare His mighty works (Psalm 145:4). In essence, mentoring, of family or other younger believers, provides us the connection that keeps the vision and mission both alive and viable across generations.

We cannot assume that the next generation automatically will understand the nature and character of Christ and how He operates unless we share. In that way, mentoring is more than a tool to share career or general life advice; it is means also to disciple newer believers and younger people. Each generation can learn about God, about godliness, about the fight for righteousness, and more from the experiences - the good and the bad - of those who have come before them. Mentoring can help the person who is being mentored to grow in faith, to avoid pitfalls, and to increase understanding of the ways of the Lord.

Throughout the Bible we find mentoring relationships. Though some may think otherwise, mentoring is not a not a new phenomenon. It is a centuries old process used for equipping the next generation. Christ was a mentor to His chosen disciples. Additionally, we see mentoring relationships such as Elijah and Elisha, Moses and Jethro, Paul and Timothy, and Naomi and Ruth. Though quite different, each relationship held significance because it provided a pathway for knowing God and His love for His people in more meaningful ways.

Elijah and Elisha

Elijah was a prophet during the rule of King Ahab, who was an evil king. God performed many miracles through Elijah - raising the dead, calling down fire from the sky, stopping the rain for three years, multiplying a widow's meager oil and flour so she and her son would not die, and more (1 Kings 17 and 18).

There came a time, though, that God instructed Elijah that he was to begin to groom his successor. God identified a young man named Elisha, who would follow him around and became a protégé of sorts (1 Kings 19:16).

After finding Elisha, Elijah did as God had directed and anointed Elisha to take his place (1 Kings 19:19-21). In preparation for his future role, Elisha traveled with Elijah, watching and experiencing along with him daily. Elisha saw Elijah perform miracles. He learned about the ways of God and observed the intimate relationship and communion Elijah had with God. He also saw, as no one else, how God worked through Elijah, and he desired to be used in that way as well. In fact, before Elijah was taken home by the Lord, he allowed Elisha to ask for anything he desired, and Elisha's request was for a double portion of his spirit. As Elijah was taken by God, Elisha received Elijah's mantle and, from God, a double portion of Elijah's spirit and power. It is recorded that Elisha began to do wonders and perform the miraculous even greater than Elijah, his mentor (2 Kings 2).

Take-Away: An effective mentor will stress that you develop an intimate relationship with God and, even more than imitating him or her, will model that you should seek the nature and character of God the Father, Son, and Holy Spirit.

Moses and Jethro

The book of Exodus tells the story of Israel's suffering in Egypt in the years after Joseph's death. However, God raised up a man named Moses to lead the children of Israel out of bondage and to the promised land. We learn, though, that despite the miracles God did for them time and again on their journey to freedom and promise, the Israelites murmured against God and disobeyed His commandments. This conduct prolonged their wilderness period for a forty-year period.

While on the journey, one of Moses's responsibilities was to serve as judge when conflicts arose among the people and to instruct them in ways of God - a role that often lasted "from morning until evening" (Exodus 18:13, NKJV). Jethro, Moses' father-in-law, observed overwhelmed Moses was with caring for the people and their concerns. God used Jethro to counsel to Moses about his approach.

***[T]his is no way to go about it. You'll burn out, and the people along with you. This is way too much for you—you can't do this alone. Now listen to me. Let me tell you how to do this so that God will be in this with you. Be there for the people before God but let the matters of concern be presented to God. Your job is to teach them the rules and*

*instructions, to show them how to live, what to do. And then you need
to keep a sharp eye out for competent men—men who fear God, men
of integrity, men who are incorruptible—and appoint them as leaders
over groups organized by the thousand, by the hundred, by fifty, and by
ten. They'll be responsible for the everyday work of judging among the
people. They'll bring the hard cases to you, but in the routine cases they'll
be the judges. They will share your load and that will make it easier for
you. If you handle the work this way, you'll have the strength to carry
out whatever God commands you, and the people in their settings will
flourish also.*

Exodus 18:17-23 (MSG)

Moses followed Jethro's instruction, and the approach worked
well going forward.

Take-Away: An effective mentor will offer insight that is both godly
and practical.

Paul and Timothy

In the New Testament, we find the Apostle Paul equipping
a young man named Timothy for the ministry. According to Acts
16:1-3, Paul met Timothy while he was traveling through Lystra.
Timothy was the son of a believing Jewess and a Greek father, and he
had an excellent reputation.

Timothy experienced Paul's mentoring in an intense way. He
traveled with Paul for over sixteen years and had the opportunity
to learn from Paul as perhaps none other. He helped Paul with
ministerial tasks, and Paul instructed him in the ways of God. Then,
during periods when Paul was imprisoned, he continued instruction
to Timothy by letter. Whether in person or in writing, Paul set the
example for Timothy of how mature ministry looks.

You, however, know all about my teaching, my way of life, my purpose, faith, patience, love, endurance, persecutions, sufferings—what kinds of things happened to me in Antioch, Iconium and Lystra, the persecutions I endured. Yet the Lord rescued me from all of them. In fact, everyone who wants to live a godly life in Christ Jesus will be persecuted, while evildoers and impostors will go from bad to worse, deceiving and being deceived. But as for you, continue in what you have learned and have become convinced of, because you know those from whom you have learned it, and how from infancy you have known the Holy Scriptures, which are able to make you wise for salvation through faith Christ Jesus.

2 Timothy 3:10-15 (NIV)

When Timothy reached about age thirty, Paul commissioned him to train other pastors and leaders until he was able to rejoin them. Timothy was much younger than the pastors, and the notion of instructing his elders was intimidating. He was apprehensive about how he would be received and somewhat uneasy about achieving the tasks he had been given. However, Paul encouraged his pupil so that he would be able to carry on the work at hand.

****I remember you in my prayers night and day, greatly desiring to see you, being mindful of your tears, that I may be filled with joy, when I call to remembrance the genuine faith that is in you, which dwelt first in your grandmother Lois and your mother Eunice, and I am persuaded is in you also. Therefore, I remind you to stir up the gift of God, which is in you, through the laying on of my hands. For God has not given us a spirit of fear, but of power and of love and of a sound mind.*

2 Timothy 1:3 – 7 (NKJV)

When Paul could not be with Timothy, he wrote letters to inspire and encourage. These letters were very personal, open, and transparent. He shared his experiences—good and bad; he reminded Timothy who he was and whose he was; and he instructed Timothy in the ways of God and how to be an effective minister and soldier for the cause of Christ.

Take-Away: An effective mentor will always encourage and inspire you.

Naomi and Ruth

The story of Naomi and Ruth is a great example of a mentoring relationship between two women. Naomi, a Judean, was living in the foreign land of Moab when her husband and two sons died. Naomi was left with her two daughters-in-law - Orpah and Ruth - both of whom were Moabites.

When a famine arose in Moab, Naomi chose to go back to Bethlehem - her homeland. Although she instructed both daughters-in-law to return to their people, Ruth refused to leave Naomi and went with her. It was clear that, over time, Naomi truly had become treasured family for Ruth, who refused to leave her "mother-in-the-Lord" to return home. The Bible recalls Ruth's eloquent message of commitment:

Don't urge me to leave you or turn back from you. Where you go, I will go, and where you stay, I will stay. Your people will be my people and your God my God. Where you die, I will die, and there I will be buried. May the Lord deal with me, be it ever so severely, if even death separates you and me.

Ruth 1:16-17 (NIV).

And, with that, Naomi stopped trying to convince Ruth otherwise. However, as we learn in the Book of Ruth, when they arrived in Bethlehem, the women were destitute and without provision. It was in this season that the Bible provides a glimpse for us into Naomi's mentoring of Ruth. She instructed the younger woman about gleaning grain in the field of Boaz - a distant relative - so that they would have food. She guided Ruth about how to determine of Boaz's interest in becoming a kinsman redeemer, as she was in need of a husband. And Naomi was there as a joyful mother-in-love as the couple married and later as they welcomed a son who would be the grandfather of David.

Ruth expressed her undying commitment to Naomi and in return, Naomi recognized that she too had been placed in a position to commit in a new way to Ruth. Naomi understood that a part of her role as a teacher to Ruth was truly to make Ruth her daughter and to help ensure that Ruth took the right path in life.

Take-Away: An effective mentor helps the mentee reach proper decisions and live out appropriate behavior when faced with challenging circumstances.

Jesus and His Disciples

There is no greater mentor than our Lord, Jesus. His example of mentorship is to be followed above all.

First of all, in Jesus's earthly ministry, He was a teacher. He did not operate a formal school or program. Instead, in three short years, He prepared, equipped, and taught His disciples the what, why, and how to continue the work He had begun. He spent time with them, knew them intimately, and nurtured their spiritual growth daily. He trained them to follow His footsteps to carry the gospel to the world. This level of instruction was essential for, if one does not know Jesus, how can he or she be an effective witness of Him?

In Christ's disciples, we also see models of those being mentored. The disciples were willing to follow Jesus and to allow Him to shape them in character and action. Their goal, whether they realized it or not, was to become like Christ. As Luke shared: "A disciple is not above his teacher, but everyone who is perfectly trained will be like his teacher" (Luke 6:40, NKJV).

Being *like* their teacher meant watching Jesus so that they could model the behavior expected of a Christ follower. Jesus's overall intent was to guide His followers into truth. We see that Jesus was a patient teacher, though, because when the disciples made mistakes, which they did and we all do, He corrected them in love and showed them the way (See, e.g., Matthew 16:5 – 12; 17: 14 – 21; or 26:36 – 46).

Jesus taught lessons with His words, and He taught lessons through His actions. Whether by word or deed, Jesus established a pattern for relationship-building and discipleship—one that we should follow. And He modeled up to the end.

When He had finished washing their feet, [H]e put on [H]is clothes and returned to [H]is place. "Do you understand what I have done for you?" He asked them. "You call [M]e 'Teacher' and 'Lord', and rightly so, for that is what I am. Now that I, your Lord and Teacher, have washed your feet, you also should wash one another's feet. I have set you an example that you should do as I have done for you. Very truly I tell you, no servant is greater than his master, nor is a messenger greater than the one who sent him. Now that you know these things, you will be blessed if you do them."

John 13:12-17 (NIV)

As the disciples followed Jesus, their lives were transformed. And even though they failed time and again, in the end they grew into whole, strong, and bold followers of Christ.

Take-Away: An effective mentor imitates Jesus. He or she sets an example, answers questions, addresses needs, provides encouragement, all in an effort to help the person develop an intimate relationship with God.

Note that mentorship is not an overnight process. It takes an investment of time and patience from the mentor and from the person being mentored. The process through which a seasoned believer passes on experience and utilizes wisdom and guidance as one younger or newer to the faith seeks to achieve a God-given mission and vision is just that—a process. The process is built on relationship and opportunity, in the ordinary and ongoing parts of life, to share and engage with each other on a regular basis.

Insight for One Desiring to Have a Mentor

My first note is that I pray that you truly desire a mentor. As you grow, there should be someone to whom you look for guidance and insight - someone who has walked where you wish to go, someone who has lived a life - through good times and bad, successes and failures - who can speak truth to you based on what has been learned over the years.

Do not refuse the counsel of your mentor. He or she is not perfect; rather that person is a gift from God to equip you for the work of the ministry. With such support, you get to learn and grow; you have a partner for ideas and thinking. This, indeed, is a blessing.

Additionally, though, having a mentor can be a much-needed resource in the tough times. Trust me, ministry work is not easy; periods will come when you will need counsel. As you move out in faith to fulfill your assignment, understand that there will be opposition. When you are the business of expanding God's kingdom and harvesting souls, Satan will oppose you. Think back to Jesus's comments to Peter:

Simon, stay on your toes. Satan has tried his best to separate all of you from [M]e, like chaff from wheat. Simon, I've prayed for you in particular that you not give in or give out. When you have come through the time of testing, turn to your companions, and give them a fresh start.

Luke 22:31-32 (MSG)

Understand that, when you enlist in God's army, you are in a battle. Preparation and training are necessary, and your mentor can play a significant role not only in providing counsel but also by interceding for you in prayer. No army intends for its soldiers to go to war alone. Consider your mentor like your personal war counsel who is in place to share biblical principles to guide you on your path.

Insight for One Enlisted as a Mentor

Just as it is important for young people to desire to identify a trusted mentor, each of us should be in a position to grow sufficiently in our faith walk that we are prepared to mentor another. In Titus Chapter 2, the Bible describes the qualities of a sound church, which include older men and women, who have established patterns of righteous living that permit them to share in ways that equip those coming behind them in the faith (vv. 1-8).

However, please do not enter a mentoring relationship as a know-it-all. You are there to guide and support, not to rule. Your job is to point the person you are mentoring to God and His way, not you and yours.

Also recognize that God is depositing in that person, just as He is communicating with you. It may surprise you that young people hear from God too and have visions from Him. God will use them mightily in this hour. And God's plan for the person you are mentoring may be quite different from His plan for you or from what you expect. We saw this vividly in the Bible as God instructed the Prophet Samuel to go to Jesse's family and anoint the next king of Israel. Samuel was certain that Eliab was the son to be anointed, but God had other plans. "Do not consider his appearance or his height, for I have rejected him. The Lord does not look at the things people look at. People look at the outward appearance, but the Lord looks at the heart" (1 Samuel 16:7). With that instruction, Samuel, led by God's Spirit, examined each of Jesse's sons until he reached David—the least likely of them all. At that point, the choice was sealed. "Then the Lord said, 'Rise and anoint him; this is the one'" (1 Samuel 16:12,NIV). And we know that David, that least-likely choice, was described as a man after God's own heart (Acts 13:22).

Also remember that, as a mentor, your words have power. They can build up, or they can break the spirit, suppress dreams, and destroy their potential. So, approach each contact gently, lovingly, and with grace. Help the person you are mentoring to develop patience, endurance, and faith to navigate current or future challenges. Share wisdom that allows the person to grasp God's seasons and timing and that adds to his or her enthusiasm and zeal for God and his charge.

Again, God did not create us to live this life alone.

Two people are better off than one, for they can help each other succeed. If one person falls, the other can reach out and help. But someone who falls alone is in real trouble. Likewise, two people lying close together can keep each other warm. But how can one be warm alone? A person standing alone can be attacked and defeated, but two can stand back-to-back and conquer. Three are even better, for a triple-braided cord is not easily broken.

Ecclesiastes 4:9-12 (NLT)

Why have I chosen to dedicate this chapter to the subject of intergenerational transfer and mentoring? We all need someone to come along side to teach, counsel, cheer, and sometimes guide us through life's joyous and challenging situations. We all need a Naomi or Paul in our life. We were not created to travel this life alone. When Jesus called the disciples to service, He called twelve and not one, and gave them a mission to fulfill. Each follower of Christ, even today, has a mission—one with which there will be greater success if we do not attempt to accomplish it solo.

So, partnering - seasoned and young - is important for individual success but is also important to the Church as a whole. People without a guidepost will get lost. If the next generation is lost, the Church's mission -carrying out the Great Commission - will be hindered. Scripture tells us that, "[w]hen people do not accept divine guidance, they run wild. But whoever obeys the law is joyful" (Proverbs 29:18, NLT). Mentoring relationships provide paths for intergenerational knowledge to be transferred to the next generation. They also provide the opportunity for both generations to work together to advance the cause of Christ—seeing God's kingdom come and His will be done on earth as it is in Heaven.

A Prayer to Partnership

Father, please raise up mature believers - men and women - whom You are equipping with the many characteristics and qualities they will need to be role models for those who are coming behind them. Let them be examples in word and in deed, gracious, transparent, humble, and generous with their time and talent, to build into the one or the ones whom You send their way and always to point them to You.

And, Father, please make each of your children hungry for guidance and wisdom. Help each one to identify the right mentor - one who will complement him or her - so that the relationship will bear the fruit of growth.

Please use these relationships to enhance the lives of both individuals through two-way sharing that models the way Christ, and His disciples did life together. And, let each encounter bring both people closer to You. In the name of Jesus, the Mentor of all mentors we pray, Amen

Chapter 6
The Dawning of a New Day

"Darkness cannot drive out darkness: only light can do that."

Dr. Martin Luther King, Jr.

Though we are in the midst of stress and strain, as I write this book, I actually am excited and full of joy at this moment of time. The reason for hope, despite the despair, is that this is a pivotal time for the Church. The silence of God is about to break, and we are about to hear His roar. He is about to do a new thing, as He releases His righteous generation and establishes His unshakeable kingdom in the earth.

With all of this shaking, God is giving us, the Church, the opportunity for a new beginning and a promising future. In many ways, we have become wayward. We have been a blessed country, and those of us who follow Christ are a chosen people. Yet, for many, our hearts have cooled towards God and the things He cares about.

Our wandering parallels that of the tribe of Ephraim - a tribe of Israel whom God loved tenderly, but that spurned Him and went after other gods. We read in the Book of Hosea not only about the undying love Hosea held for his wayward wife Gomer, but the Bible demonstrates God's tenderness for His wayward Ephraim. God taught the people of Ephraim how to walk, nurtured them, removed the yoke of bondage from their necks, and healed them, but still they refused to repent and turn to God. As a result, they were chastened by God because they refused to return and exalt the One who loved them so desperately.

Much like Ephraim, America and the Church also has refused to repent for turning its back on God - for atrocities done in the name of the Lord, for unloving and unfair treatment others, and for a range of other outright acts of sin. God has been merciful and gracious even though, in many ways, we too have played the harlot and compromised with the world. Oh, I am so thankful that God is longsuffering, forgiving, and empathetic to our human condition. He takes no pleasure in chastening us; however, His patience does have an end. If we do not repent, He will discipline us. "[T]he Lord disciplines the one [H]e loves and [H]e chastens everyone [H]e accepts as [H]is son" (Hebrews 12:6, NIV). His correction does not stem from a heart of meanness or as an attempt to harm us; He, our good Father, corrects because He sees us heading in the wrong direction and wants us to discontinue our sinful ways. He loves His people, and His love is everlasting. He is merciful and faithful. And, because of His faithful love for us, He is giving us a chance to return to Him.

Prophecies of doom and gloom have been around forever. That is not the intent here. With that said, though let me be clear, we are in the end times and Christ's return is eminent (Matthew 4:30). But this same God "is patient toward you, not wanting anyone to perish, but everyone to come to repentance" (2 Peter 3:9). That's why I can share with you that God is not finished with the Church, with America, or with the rest of the world. Yes, the signs all around us are pointing to Christ's coming, but clearly His bride - the Church - isn't ready. There is still much work to be done to prepare us to receive our returning Jesus. And so, the Spirit of the Lord is at work turning things around. God is busy cleansing and purifying His Church. COVID, unrest, hurricanes, wildfires, and the like are God shaking us and inviting us to get ready. Oh, may we be like the wise virgins in Matthew 25, who had lamps filled with oil and who were ready for the bridegroom's return rather than those who were foolish and unprepared when He came back.

Christ desires a glorious Church when He returns. His plans have not changed. First, though, there must come repentance, and repentance must begin with the Church. If God's people will but pray, humble themselves, turn from their wicked ways, repent, and seek His face, God promised that we will hear from heaven and healing and restoration will come (2 Chronicles 7:14). As we seek scientific answers to COVID-19 and climate change, legal, policy, and humanitarian responses to injustice, we still must also realize we won't turn the corner on any of these issues facing our world unless and until the Church repents. We must confess the many ways we have dishonored God and put our selfish priorities above our kingdom assignment. And we must repent for taking advantage of God's grace and mercy. Despite our sinfulness He has been so good to us. Despite our sinfulness, He has held back and has not given us truly what we deserve.

Go back to the 2 Chronicles passage. Heaven hearing us and healing us rest on the actions of God's people. Until the Church repents and returns to the Lord, don't expect real change; in fact, things may get worse. The Church holds the compass of our world. The earth has been placed in our hands to manage. In Genesis 1:26-30, God entrusted mankind with dominion over the earth. This dominion charge wasn't given to simply put us in control; we were called to fill the earth with His glory because we were made in His image - an image that was designed to fill a space that formerly was in chaos and darkness and to create a kingdom culture that represented our Father. Through Christ, we became God's children (John 1:12-13). We, however, have done a rather sloppy job in fulfilling the assignments God has given us. And so, He is shaking all of His children to get us back on track.

The reality is that some of us though sealed for eternity by Christ's blood, will not have the joy of being a true part of His earthly ministry. While some of us won't make a meaningful kingdom-building contribution, God will not allow His ultimate purpose to falter. He always has a ram in the bush, and one of His current rams is the new generation that He is preparing - a new generation of righteous leaders and believers who are being groomed to accomplish His will.

Through this generation, reformation will come. Through them, our churches will become true houses of prayer, where the Holy Spirit has preeminence and where disciples are made and multiplied. Lives will be transformed and conformed to the image of Christ, filled with the Holy Spirit.

Such an environment will usher in the manifested sons and daughters of God, born of His Spirit. The Church will emerge bolder, stronger, and powerful than ever before. This will be the defining hour - the greatest hour – of the Church. The world will witness the unshakeable kingdom of God exhibited through the manifestation of sons and daughters who truly represent the Father well.

In conclusion, let me ask you two questions:

Question 1: Are you ready to repent?

All of us are in need of repentance. Repentance is more than just asking for forgiveness or acknowledging sin. At the core of repentance is a truly heart change. King David reminds us that God does not delight so much in the outward signs of repentance, such as making a sacrifice, but "[t]he sacrifices of God are a broken spirit, [a] broken and contrite heart—These, O God, You will not despise (Psalm 51:16-17).

The greatest sin of the Church is relational. We grieve God's heart immeasurably when we turn away from Him and become lukewarm in our love. We break relationship when we go our own way without considering Him. We go astray when we forget who He is and who we are to Him (Revelation 3:14-17). The good news is that, although we may drift, God is relentless. Returning to Revelation 3, He shares that "as many as I love, I rebuke and chasten. Therefore, be zealous and repent. Behold, I stand at the door and knock. If anyone hears My voice and opens the door, I will come into him and dine with him, and he with Me" (vv19 – 20). *Remember, there is always the opportunity to rekindle our relationship with God - our first love.*

Question 2: Are you willing to surrender your life totally to God and to devote yourself wholly to doing His will?

When you come to Christ, you have a choice. Will you surrender to Christ or keep doing things your own way? Certainly, there is the initial surrender that occurs at the time you give your life to Christ and accept salvation. However, God also seeks a second type of surrender - one that is equally important. He wants you to surrender to His Lordship; that is, He wants you to defer to His leading over your mind, will, and body. Such surrender isn't losing who you are. Instead, it's gaining - taking on His life and, in so doing, relinquishing the control of your life to Him. Apostle Paul sums it up this way: "[I]t is no longer I who live, but Christ lives in me; and the life which I live in the flesh I live by faith in the Son of God, who loved me and gave Himself for me" (Galatians 2:20). As counterintuitive as that may sound, if you are willing to give the whole of your life to Christ and make His kingdom agenda your priority, you will find that you gain far more than you lose.

We are approaching uncharted territory and the dawning of a new day. The Church has been brought to its knees. There is no mistake who is in control. The message is clear; God desires a generation after His own heart—one that will finish the work that Christ started.

The Holy Spirit is at work. He is birthing a new generation - people after God's heart, a group that will honor Christ as its head and the Holy Spirit as administrator of Christ's Church. God is readying the bride of Christ for the return of the bridegroom. He is raising up a generation that will execute His plans, obey His voice, and glorify Him. He is preparing a Church that will demonstrate the living Christ to the world by the way we love Him, the way we live and by the way we love one another (John 13:34 – 35). Then, we will experience open windows of heaven, glory of His Kingdom, the dawning of a new day for the Church and the world.

My Prayer for You

I pray that the Holy Spirit will keep you from falling and present you before Jesus at His coming without fault.

I pray that He will unveil within you the unlimited riches of His glory and the dynamic power of the Holy Spirit who resides in you.

I pray that, in His name, the unsaved will be drawn to the saving grace of Christ and, if you already are His child, that the unsaved around you will see Christ in you in such a genuine way that they are changed by your living testimony.

I pray that His love takes root in your heart and your thoughts, that it will be spoken from your lips, and that you overflow with the endless love for the humanity for which Christ died.

I pray that you rise up and shine your light, and I pray that you devote time to your relationship with God that you become the salt of the earth.

I pray that God will tap you as a part of this generation - a soldier who will rise up in the power of the Holy Spirit and do the impossible and extraordinary.

I pray that you will arm yourself daily in God's mighty armor so that you will be kept from the evil one and surrounded with protection by God's holy angel army.

Finally, I pray that you will be bold, courageous, and strong as a lion as you boldly proclaim the gospel to the glory of God and the building up of His kingdom. Amen

God's New Z Generation Arising
The Spoken Word

In conclusion, I would like to share the spoken words from the Z generation arising. These words spoken demonstrate the hearts of the emerging generation God is raising up in this time.

God's New Z Generation Arising

by Matthew McCluskey

America! A new wave is rising. A movement of young people, supported by the older generations, bound together in honor.

A new generation, which will not be content to passively sit in church pews. We will not allow what the culture has labeled us by the secular propaganda to influence how we love, but we will destroy every false accusation against us by revealing true love.

For we are a movement of Love -- a Love that flows from the Father's heart, brave enough to lose its life to see others set free. We will love people enough to call out their self-destructive thinking patterns, and we will declare holy truth to bring freedom to our generation.

We are a generation which will contend to bring forth our Father's kingdom. We are a generation which believes that the best years of the Church in America are still to come. We are a generation which will contend and work for generations yet unborn.

We are a generation not just focused on revival, but reformation of every part of our society. We are a generation which will live faithful to Jesus unto DEATH. We're no longer slaves to the empty opinions of a bankrupt culture and the immature members of our generation.

And, we reject the washed-up and failed philosophies which were taught to us in school of humanism, socialism, and the cultural degeneracy. But, being sons, not just in name, but with our Father's love, forming the foundation of every thought -- we move forward boldly, seizing moments in time to show off real beauty -- the beauty of Jesus.

We are a generation that will grow up, intimately experiencing the Holy Spirit and feeling the deepest embrace of His love -- and will learn to love like He loves. We are a generation of worshippers who will now go to war.

And, bring His Kingdom wherever we are, in every place of society. We do not seek a truce or peace with this society. We seek to win entirely. We seek to conquer in His name, with His love, by His blood, and by His power.

The future belongs to us. To us -- the Spirit-filled millennials, to us -- Generation Z. This is a revolution of every young believer, beginning to rise up for the world to see the glory and splendor of our King.

The time is now, so arise, and press toward the prize of the high call!

After Thought: A Call to Love and Prayer

While waiting for the last edits of this book, I became concerned and disturbed about the political climate, the civil unrest and uprising now existing in our country. Never in my lifetime have I seen such divisiveness and, in some respects, downright hatred.

Although I know that such things are to be expected in a world that does not know Christ, it still has been difficult to witness. It is hard to see the Church behaving as it has. Pastors and congregations stand unapologetically in opposition to one another because of political candidates and current events. What's happening now is surreal. And, if it all causes *my* heart to ache, I can't imagine how it grieves the heart of our Father.

Step back for a moment, though. Look with spiritual eyes. If you do, you will see just the type of spiritual wickedness in high places, stemming from principalities, and designed by the ruler of this world's darkness, written about in Ephesians 6:12. Satan and his demons have taken control over many in our government and have seduced them into believing that they are not subject to God, the Almighty. They, and too many of us, have placed faith in men instead of in God the Creator, the all-powerful One, who can form something out of nothing simply by His spoken word, the stroke of His hand, or breath from His nostrils.

There is a dark cloud over our country because the Church refuses to honor and submit to God. Sadly, the difference between the world and the Church, at times, is indistinguishable. Visit online postings, and it is as common to see believers spewing hate, lies, and distortions in the same manner as those who do not know our Savior. Members of Christ's body seem to be as prone to trust men over God and to hold up idols in much the same way that the world does.

While such thinking and behavior compromises our witness, it does far more. It actually puts us at odds with God. Never should we prefer man or law over God and the law of love. God was very clear. "Thou shall have no other gods before Me" (Exodus 20:2, NKJV). We have been called to love the Lord our God with all of our heart, soul, and mind (Deuteronomy 6:5; Matthew 22:37-38). That, Jesus told us, is the greatest commandment. However, He followed it with a second that He held as being just as important. We are to love our neighbor as we love ourselves (Matthew 22:39-40). If we do not love God *and* love the people He created, we can offer sacrifices or follow every law on the books, and it means nothing.

Am I advocating that we not obey the law? No. However, laws and man can never change a heart; only Christ can.

The world has a sin problem. Abortionists have a sin problem. Racists have a sin problem. Adulterers have a sin problem. Looters have a sin problem. Liars have a sin problem. And the sin list goes on. We ALL have a sin problem, and only Christ has the answer for our sin. We should be thankful that the sin issue already has been settled by the love of God that allowed Christ's sacrifice of shed blood to pay our sin debt and extend eternal life to all who accept His gift.

However, as the Apostle Paul wrote to the Roman church, "[s]hall we continue to sin that grace may abound? Certainly not (Romans 6:1-2, NKJV)!" We can't flippantly take advantage of God's grace and mercy in that way - by knowingly sinning and being hard-hearted and expecting Him to just accept our sin and us. God doesn't want us to be like the world; He wants us to be transformed truly into His children who demonstrate His perfect will to the world (Romans 12:2).

Above all, we must remember that it is the love of God that covers all sin. And, in obvious ways, what the world needs now is to see the love of God demonstrated by Christ's Church.

The answer to the problems we're facing is not political or legislative or social; it's spiritual. God is concerned about the hearts of men. Because that's God's concern, it also should be our concern. The Church's purpose is to represent the kingdom of God and to bring His love to our sin-sick world, a world craving the presence of God, a world in need of a heart transplant. Even God's people will never be able to change the world by relying on the flesh. God is the only One who can heal our land.

The Church has gotten it all wrong.

Our focus should not be on politics and power. In this hour, we have been called to pray, to love, and to act in accordance with God's directive. As I mentioned earlier in this book, there is no greater weapon in our arsenal than prayer. Want to see change? Pray. God intervenes when we pray. Scripture reveals that God's eyes are on the righteous and His ears are attentive to their prayers (1 Peter 3:12). We know that whatever we ask for in prayer and in belief, we will receive (Mark 11:24). Jesus told those who followed Him that He would do whatever they asked in His Name so that the Father would be glorified through Him - the Son (John 14:13). John assures us that we can have confidence in approaching God because, if we ask anything according His will, He hears us and, because He hears us, He will grant our petitions (1 John 5:14-15).

However, the promises of prayer are not without boundary. It is the effectual and fervent prayers of the righteous that avail - or yield - much, not just any prayer. Also, we can't forget who we are and who God is. God was quite clear that the people, called by His Name, would have audience with Him on the condition that we humble ourselves, pray, seek His face, and turn from our wicked ways. When we take these actions, then He will hear from heaven, forgive, and heal our land (2 Chronicles 7:14). An annual day of prayer is not what moves the hand of God. A haughty spirit or refusal to seek righteousness is not what equips us with the Holy

Spirit's power to defeat the enemy. Prayerful submission is our only recourse.

The prophet Elijah is example of what prayer can do. At God's direction, He prayed earnestly that it would not rain, and no rain fell on the land for three and a half years. Yet, when God led, he prayed again, the rain came, and fruitfulness was restored to the land (James 5:17-18). Similarly, think back to Paul and Silas, in prison and praising God at midnight. Suddenly, an earthquake shook the foundations of the prison, and everyone's prison chains were loosed (Acts 16:25-26). True prayer has power!

Imagine what would happen if the Church would commit to setting aside time to pray for the salvation of sinners. Because salvation for all certainly is God's will (John 3:16; 2 Peter 3:9), there is no doubt that, in response to such prayers, God would move, chains would be broken, and people would be loosed from the power of sin. When we pray, we welcome God's entrance into the affairs of our hearts, our circumstances, and the things that matter to Him. That's not just my thinking; we see it illustrated for us in Scripture. Paul and the disciples devoted themselves to prayer, asking the Lord to open hearts to the gospel message, and we see the number of believers increasing exponentially (Acts 16:5, 13-15). God's call for prayer is still vital today if we want Him to move in us and in the world around us.

So, we've missed the mark on prayer. The Church also has missed the mark on love.

Jesus said that we are to love one another, just as He has loved us and that this type of love would be what marked us as His disciples to an onlooking world (John 13:34-35). He didn't say love only whites, Hispanics, Asians, or Blacks. He said love one another—period; and, when others see us loving this way, they will know that we belong to Christ and both see and be open to receiving His love.

If anyone boasts, "I love God," and goes right on hating his brother or sister, thinking nothing of it, he is a liar. If he won't love the person he can see, how can he love the God he can't see? The command we have from Christ is blunt: Loving God includes loving people. You've got to love both.

1 John 4:20 (MSG)

Jesus loved all people—all races, all backgrounds, all economic statuses. If we truly have accepted Christ as Savior, He has implanted His Holy Spirit in us, which means that we have that same capacity to love (1 John 4:16).

At times it may be challenging to love, especially those whom we deem undesirable. Christ understood that, but He didn't change the command. We are called to love. Anyone who doesn't love the person right in front of him, cannot sincerely know and love God because God *is* love (1 John 4:8). In those hard-to-love situations, focusing on the difficulty of loving or the problem with the other person is counterproductive. Instead, we must remind ourselves of God's love for us - love that transcends our faults and that provides us with the unmerited gift of grace for our redemption. God's way is love and, because we are His, it should be our way too.

If I speak with human eloquence and angelic ecstasy but don't love, I'm nothing but the creaking of a rusty gate.

If I speak God's Word with power, revealing all [H]is mysteries and making everything plain as day, and if I have faith that says to a mountain, "Jump," and it jumps, but I don't love, I'm nothing.

If I give everything I own to the poor and even go to the stake to be burned as a martyr, but I don't love, I've gotten nowhere. So, no matter what I say, what I believe, and what I do, I'm bankrupt without love.

1 Corinthians 13:1-3 (MSG)

We cannot get around this call to love. Nothing we do—marching, protesting, pushing legislative agendas, preaching, posting on social media, nothing—can take the place of love, which is the greatest charge of all (1 Corinthians 13:13). When any of us comes face-to-face with God in eternity, it is highly unlikely that He will be concerned with the trappings. He will ask what we have done with His love? Have we loved one another so that others can see us clearly as His disciples - the vessels of His love?

In closing, the Spirit of the Lord instructed me to pass along this message to His Church and especially to the leaders of the faith:

I never told you pursue court seats in order to change the laws and the course of a nation to bring about righteousness in the land. I am God. I do not need you to fight My battles. I am the Creator of the entire universe, including the earth and everything and everybody that dwells on it. Nothing is too hard for Me to do. I told you to preach the gospel, pray and to love people. You moved forward, pursuing your own agenda but never did you consult with Me about whether this should be done.

I see what you see; in fact, I see far more than you ever could see. I know what to do. I know the end from the beginning. You are trying to exert your muscle of flesh in order to pursue an agenda. But, in your flesh alone you cannot succeed, and you will never stand in My glory. Only I will receive the glory.

I am a God of love. I ask of you just two things - be the light of the world and show forth My love. Do that and, through you, I will do wonders in your world. However, what you are doing on your own cannot change the hearts of men; in many respects, it infuriates them. I created those around you; I, and I alone, know what will move them. My desire is for all people to experience the love of Jesus Christ. But, when you fail to hear Me or seek to understand My ways, you just get in the way.

I have called you pray. Communing with Me allows you to get to know Me. Prayer also moves My hands and provides a fertile setting for Me to touch hearts. Softening a heart of stone is within My exclusive power, not yours; I simply invite you to be an instrument in the process by introducing My love to others in human form.

I'm not interested in your outward expressions of righteousness, when inwardly your heart really is made of stone and filled with hatred. I am not interested in your stances and positions, unless they have been inspired by Me and are personifications of My love. Your independent acts do not interest Me in the least.

I am love, but I also am a God of judgement. And I will judge My Church if it will not walk in love and to do what I called it to do.

Today's world condition is a sin condition, and you have a lot to do with where the world finds itself today. I asked you to pray in order to stop the hands of the enemy, and you did not. If you had prayed, prayer would not have been taken out of the school. If you had prayed, where violence now reigns, there would be peace. If you had prayed and sought My face, evil and drugs would not have consumed lives and families in cities, suburbs, and rural communities. If you had prayed, My heart would not weep daily from the murder of babies in the womb. If you had prayed, the divisiveness among races, and classes, and ideologies would not exist because you all would know that everyone has been made in My image. If you had prayed....

But pray you did not. And now the world is suffering the consequences. Your prayers would have led to a mighty outpouring of the Holy Spirit, and the world right now would know My love. Instead, you have gone to men to plead your cause—men who have never had my heart. But, because you have desired them, your desire has been granted. And now, look at the death and destruction brought to your land as a result. They have amplified the spirit of anti-Christ in your land- spirit of death, destruction and chaos. They have partnered with nations that hate Me and My Son. Yet, you solute them, follow them, and either ignore or encourage their sinful acts. Recognize that they are mere men. They can be flushed away by one breath from My nostril. They would not be standing if I did not allow it. And I allowed it because this is your desire - them, and not Me. They have become your God and you love them rather than Me.

You tout patriotism. You raise your flags of red, white, and blue, but where is My flag—the flag of righteousness, justice, and love that proclaims the Prince of Peace.

Oh, if you had acknowledged and called upon Me, I would have answered, intervened, and showed you wonderful and mighty things. But now because of your actions, you are reaping the whirlwind. Your hand has been stained with innocent blood and intertwined with hatred of degenerates and their destructive behavior. You would have had more than you could ever ask or imagine because I am God and I lavish good on My own. I am God and I am good, and I desire that my people to know Me. I want Mine to know that, when they come to Me and pray according to My will, all things are possible.

My beloved, it is late, but it is not too late. I am looking for opportunities to show you how much I love you. I have given you prayer, a way to interact with Me anytime and anyplace. It is perhaps the greatest gift that I could give except for Myself, My Son, and My Holy Spirit.

Having already received so much, will you not repent and turn back to me? I am the one that opens and closes doors without trickery and manipulation. I am the one who grants grace and favor because of Who I Am and who my Son is. I do not need your money to influence world decisions. I only need you to cry out to Me in prayer on the behalf of your country. Watch me act and watch me show mercy. Am I not God Almighty, the God who is Omniscient and Omnipotent?

Will you not bring glory to My name by sharing My love to the world and demonstrating to them that I AM Almighty God and that nothing is impossible for Me? I can change the hearts of men; after all, I changed yours!

I have not called for the end of days yet, because there are more to be saved and there is a Church that still unprepared. But I have sent this message to remind you of what I asked you to do. Your task now is to get right with Me yourself and, as you do, to pray for the salvation and sanctification of those around you; be my true disciples, My light in darkness and show the world my Love.

Return to Me and get yourself out of the way so that My love can be poured into you and also out through you. Then the world will know of My kingdom of righteousness, justice, peace, and love - not just any love, but MY Love.

Acknowledgements

I am grateful and thankful to June Mickens my editor for her contributions to this book. She knows my heart, my spirit and is connected with the heart of God. A special thanks to my niece, Tiffany for her review of the manuscript and recommended changes. Thank you my "Come Away with Me Zoom" group, my sister LaVonne, and Michelle for your prayers and support.

Bible Citations

Introduction

1. Be still and know that I am God; I will be exalted among the nations; I will be exalted in the earth!" (Psalms 46:10, NKJV)

Chapter 1- The Shaking Continues

1. So, don't turn a deaf ear to these gracious words. If those who ignored earthly warnings didn't get away with it, what will happen to us if we turn our backs on heavenly warnings? His voice that time shook the earth to its foundations; this time—[H]e's told us this quite plainly—[H]e'll also rock the heavens: "One last shaking, from top to bottom, stem to stern." The phrase "one last shaking" means a thorough housecleaning, getting rid of all the historical and religious junk so that the unshakable essentials stand clear and uncluttered.

2. Do you see what we've got? An unshakable kingdom! And do you see how thankful we must be? Not only thankful, but brimming with worship, deeply reverent before God. For God is not an indifferent bystander. He's actively cleaning house, torching all that needs to burn, and [H]e won't quit until all is cleansed. God [H]himself is Fire! (Hebrews 12:25-29, MSG)

3. And if judgement begins with us, what terrible fate awaits those who have never obeyed God's Good News?" (1 Peter 4:17, NLT)

4. Second Corinthians 13:5-8 explains it this way: "Test yourselves to make sure you are solid in the faith. Don't drift along taking everything for granted. Give yourselves regular checkups

5. When it rained and rained and the flood came, with wind and waves beating upon his house, it collapsed and was swept away. (Matthew 7:24-27, TPT)

6. Maybe this time of silence will awaken us, and like King David, we will proclaim that, "[a]s the deer pants [longingly] for the water brooks, [s]o my soul pants [longingly] for You, O God. My soul [my life, my inner self] thirsts for God, for the living God." (Psalm 42:1-2, AMP)

Chapter 2- Everything Is Changing: The Birth of a New Generation

1. There is a time for everything,

and a season for every activity under the heavens:

a time to be born and a time to die,

a time to plant and a time to uproot,

a time to kill and a time to heal,

a time to tear down and a time to build,

a time to weep and a time to laugh,

a time to mourn and a time to dance,

a time to scatter stones and a time to gather them,

a time to embrace and a time to refrain from embracing,

a time to search and a time to give up,

a time to keep and a time to throw away,

a time to tear and a time to mend,

a time to be silent and a time to speak,

a time to love and a time to hate,

a time for war and a time for peace.

(Ecclesiastes 3:1-8, NIV)

Chapter 3- Enters a Generation after God's Own Heart

1. We will tell the next generation the praiseworthy deeds of the LORD, [H]is power, and the wonders [H]e has done. He decreed statutes for Jacob and established the law in Israel, which [H]e commanded our ancestors to teach their children, so the next generation would know them, even the children yet to be born, and they in turn would tell their children. (Psalm 78:4-6, NIV)

2. I'm establishing [M]y covenant between [M]e and you, a covenant that includes your descendants, a covenant that goes on and on and on, a covenant that commits [M]e to be your God and the God of your descendants" (Genesis 17:7, MSG).

3. Arise, shine; for your light has come,

   and the glory of the LORD rises upon you.

   See, darkness will cover the earth

   and thick darkness is over the peoples,

   but the LORD rises upon you

   and [H]is glory appears over you.

   Nations will come to your light,

   and kings to the brightness of your dawn.

Lift up your eyes and look about you:

All assemble and come to You;

your sons come from afar,

and your daughters are carried on the hip.

Then you will look and be radiant,

your heart will throb and swell with joy;

the wealth of the seas will be brought to you,

to you the riches of the nations will come. (Isaiah 60:1-5, NIV)

4. God's Spirit would fall upon *all* flesh, not only on the sons and daughters of believers, but on *all* flesh, every kind of people. And, when that occurs, our sons and daughters will prophesy (Joel 2:28) In Judges chapter 3, the Bible tells us that "[t]he children of Israel again did evil in the sight of the Lord. So, the Lord strengthened Egon the king of Moab against Israel, because they had done evil in the sight of the Lord" (v. 12).

5. What they have meant for evil, God will turn around for good (Genesis 50:20). God wants justice—oceans of it. He wants fairness—rivers of it (Amos 5:24). Our God loves righteousness and justice and, ultimately, He will see it prevail (Psalms 33:5).

Chapter 4- The Army of the Lord Arising

1. Do not be afraid or discouraged because of this vast army. For the battle is not yours, but God's. Tomorrow march down against them. *** You will not need to fight in this battle. Take up your positions; stand firm and see the deliverance the LORD will give you, Judah and Jerusalem. Do not be afraid; do not be discouraged. Go out to face them tomorrow, and

the LORD will be with you. (vv. 15-17)

2. We are to "pray without ceasing" (1 Thessalonians 5:17, NKJV).

3. He sought God in prayer and fasting, crying out for many days in repentance for mercy and help (Nehemiah 1:4).

4. (See, e.g., Matthew 14:23 and 26:36; Mark 6:46 and 13:33; Luke 6:12 and 9:28; and John 14:16.) Jesus prayed in the morning and at night. He prayed before He raised Lazarus from the dead (John 11:41-42). Before His ascension He prayed for Himself, for His disciples, and for all of us who would come after them (John 17).

5. Whenever you pray, be sincere and not like the pretenders who love the attention they receive while praying before others in the meetings and on street corners. Believe [M]e, they've already received in full their reward. But whenever you pray, go into your innermost chamber and be alone with Father God, praying to [H]im in secret. And your Father, who sees all you do, will reward you openly. When you pray, there is no need to repeat empty phrases, praying like those who don't know God, for they expect God to hear them because of their many words. There is no need to imitate them, since your Father already knows what you need before you ask [H]im.

6. Pray like this:

"Our Father, dwelling in the heavenly realms,
may the glory of [Y]our name
be the center on which our lives turn.
Manifest [Y]our kingdom realm,
and cause [Y]our every purpose to be fulfilled on earth,

just as it is fulfilled in heaven.

We acknowledge [Y]ou as our Provider

of all we need each day.

Forgive us the wrongs we have done as we ourselves

release forgiveness to those who have wronged us.

Rescue us every time we face tribulation

and set us free from evil.

For [Y]ou are the King who rules

with power and glory forever. Amen" (Matthew 6:5-13, TPT)

7. I will declare Your name to my brethren; In the midst of the assembly I will sing praise to You" (Hebrews 2:12, NKJV).

8. He gathered the people, proclaimed a fast, and reached out to God through praise and worship (2 Chronicles 20:1-4).

9. Lord, the God of our ancestors, are [Y]ou not the God who is in heaven? You rule over all kingdoms and nations. Power and might are in [Y]our hand, and no one can withstand [Y]ou (2 Chronicles 20:6 NIV). Give thanks to the LORD, for [H]is love endures forever" (v. 21). The Bible tells us that, "[a]s they began to sing and to praise, the LORD set ambushes against the men of Ammon and Moab and Mount Seir who were invading Judah, and they were defeated" (v.22).

10. —"to go and make disciples of all nations, baptizing them in the name of the Father and of the Son and of the Holy Spirit, and teaching them to obey everything [Christ has] commanded" (Matthew 28:19 – 20, NIV).

11. However, we are told in Ephesians 6:12 (NKJV) that "we do not wrestle against flesh and blood, but against principalities, against powers, against the rulers of the darkness of this age, against spiritual hosts of wickedness in the heavenly places".

12. Jesus knew the spirit of anti-Christ would come and that His followers would be persecuted. In fact, Jesus told His disciples they would have trouble in this but to take heart that He had overcome the world (John 16:33).

13. [T]he Master selected seventy and sent them ahead of [H]im in pairs to every town and place where [H]e intended to go. ***The seventy came back triumphant. "Master, even the demons danced to your tune!" Jesus said, "I know. I saw Satan fall, a bolt of lightning out of the sky. See what I've given you? Safe passage as you walk on snakes and scorpions, and protection from every assault of the [e]nemy. No one can put a hand on you. (Luke 10:1, 17-19, MSG)

14. And take the mighty razor-sharp Spirit-sword, of the spoken Word of God. (Ephesians 6:10-18, TPT)

15. Satan came to him three recorded times trying to seduce Him into following him rather than God. Each time, Jesus' rebuttal was the word of God (Luke 4:1 - 13).

16. David answered, "You come at me with sword and spear and battle-ax. I come at you in the name of God-of-the-Angel-Armies, the God of Israel's troops, whom you curse and mock. This very day God is handing you over to me. *** And everyone gathered here will learn that God doesn't save by means of sword or spear. The battle belongs to God—[H]e's handing you to us on a platter. (1 Samuel 17:38-40, 45-47, MSG)

17. The Word will not return void but will accomplish what God intended to achieve with its use (Isaiah 55:11).

Chapter 5- Intergenerational Transfer: Mentoring the Next Generation

1. God performed many miracles through Elijah—raising the dead, calling down fire from the sky, stopping the rain for three years, multiplying a widow's meager oil and flour so she and her son would not die, and more (1 Kings 17 and 18).

2. God identified a young man named Elisha, who would follow him around and became a protégé of sorts (1 Kings 19:16).

3. After finding Elisha, Elijah did as God had directed and anointed Elisha to take his place (1 Kings 19:19-21).

4. While on the journey, one of Moses' responsibilities was to serve as judge when conflicts arose among the people and to instruct them in ways of God—a role that often lasted "from morning until evening" (Exodus 18:13, NKJV). Keep each other's spirits up so that no one falls behind or drops out" (Ephesians 6:18, MSG).

5. Scripture tells us that one generation shall praise the works of Lord to another and declare His mighty works (Psalms 145:4).

6. [T]his is no way to go about it. You'll burn out, and the people along with you. This is way too much for you - you can't do this alone. Now listen to me. Let me tell you how to do this so that God will be in this with you. Be there for the people before God but let the matters of concern be presented to God. Your job is to teach them the rules and instructions, to show them how to live, what to do. And then you need to keep a sharp eye out for competent men - men who fear God, men of integrity, men who are incorruptible - and appoint them as leaders over groups organized by the thousand, by the hundred, by fifty, and by ten. They'll be responsible for

the everyday work of judging among the people. They'll bring the hard cases to you, but in the routine cases they'll be the judges. They will share your load and that will make it easier for you. If you handle the work this way, you'll have the strength to carry out whatever God commands you

7. According to Acts 16:1-3, Paul met Timothy while he was traveling through Lystra. Timothy was the son But as for you, continue in what you have learned and have become convinced of, because you know those from whom you have learned it, and how from infancy you have known the Holy Scriptures, which are able to make you wise for salvation through faith Christ Jesus. (2 Timothy 3:10-15, NIV). Son of a believing Jewess and a Greek father, and he had an excellent reputation. 6:40, NKJV).

8. Therefore, I remind you to stir up the gift of God, which is in you, through the laying on of my hands. For God has not given us a spirit of fear, but of power and of love and of a sound Don't urge me to leave you or turn back from you. Where you go, I will go, and where you stay I will stay. Your people will be my people and your God my God. Where you die, I will die, and there I will be buried. May the Lord deal with me, be it ever so severely, if even death separates you and me. (Ruth 1:16-17. NIV).

9. A disciple is not above his teacher, but everyone who is perfectly trained will be like his teacher" (Luke We see that Jesus was a patient teacher, though, because when the disciples made mistakes, which they did and we all do, He corrected them in love and showed them the way. (See, e.g., Matthew 16:5 – 12; 17: 14 – 21; or 26:36 – 46.)

10. When He had finished washing their feet, [H]e put on [H]is clothes and returned to [H]is place. "Do you understand what I have done for you?" He asked them. "You call [M]

e 'Teacher' and 'Lord', and rightly so, for that is what I am. Now that I, your Lord and Teacher, have washed your feet, you also should wash one another's feet. I have set you an example that you should do as I have done for you. Very truly I tell you, no servant is greater than his master, nor is a messenger greater than the one who sent him. Now that you know these things, you will be blessed if you do them" (John 13:12-17, NIV).

11. Satan has tried his best to separate all of you from [M]e, like chaff from wheat. Simon, I've prayed for you in particular that you not give in or give out. When you have come through the time of testing, turn to your companions and give them a fresh start. (Luke 22:31-32, MSG)

12. In Titus Chapter 2, the Bible describes the qualities of a sound church, which include older men and women, who have established patterns of righteous living that permit them to share in ways that equip those coming behind them in the faith (vv. 1-8).

13. The Lord does not look at the things people look at. People look at the outward appearance, but the Lord looks at the heart" (1 Samuel 16:7).

14. At that point, the choice was sealed. "Then the Lord said, 'Rise and anoint him; this is the one'" (1 Samuel 16:12). And we know that David, that least-likely choice, was described as a man after God's own heart (Acts 13:22).

15. Two people are better off than one, for they can help each other succeed. If one person falls, the other can reach out and help. But someone who falls alone is in real trouble. Likewise, two people lying close together can keep each other warm. But how can one be warm alone? A person standing alone can be attacked and defeated, but two can stand back-to-

back and conquer. Three are even better, for a triple-braided cord is not easily broken. (Ecclesiastes 4:9-12, NLT)

16. So, until I come, be diligent in devouring the [w]ord of God, be faithful in prayer, and in teaching the believers. (1 Timothy 4:12-13, TPT)

Chapter 6- Dawning of a New Day: Hope of the Nation Arising

1. With that said, though, I must be clear - the world is coming to end and, at some point, Christ will return (Revelation 19:11). But this same God "is patient toward you, not wanting anyone to perish, but everyone to come to repentance" (2 Peter 3:9).

2. Through Christ, we became God's children (John 1:12-13).

3. Then you will call upon Me and go and pray to Me, and I will listen to you. And you will seek Me and find Me, when you search for Me with all your heart" (Jeremiah 29:12-13).

4. "For as many as are led by the Spirit of God, these are the sons of God" (Romans 8:14, NKJV).

5. "Arise, shine; For your light has come! And the glory of the Lord is risen upon you" (Isaiah 60:1).

6. King David reminds us that God does not delight so much in the outward signs of repentance, such as making a sacrifice, but "[t]he sacrifices of God are a broken spirit, [a] broken and contrite heart—These, O God, You will not despise (Psalms 51:16-17).

7. We go astray when we forget who He is and who we are to Him (Revelation 3:14-17).

8. Apostle Paul sums this way: "[I]t is no longer I who live, but Christ lives in me; and the life which I live in the flesh I live by faith in the Son of God, who loved me and gave Himself for me" (Galatians 2:20).

9. He is preparing a Church that will demonstrate the living Christ to the world by the way we love Him and by the way we love one another (John 13:34 – 35).

10. It was his desire to have God's position, power, seat, glory, and standing that got him thrown out of heaven (Isaiah 14:12-21). And today he still is competing for the worship and honor that only God deserves.

11. We read in Judges 3:10 (NKJV) that "[t]he Spirit of the LORD came upon [Othniel], and he judged Israel". Scripture relates how Samuel shared God's word with Saul, advising him that "the Spirit of the LORD will come upon you, and you will prophesy...and be turned into another man" (1 Samuel 10:6, NKJV). We learn that the Spirit descended as a dove upon Jesus as He began His ministry (Matthew 3:16).

12. Judges 3:10 (NKJV) that "[t]he Spirit of the LORD came upon [Othniel], and he judged Israel." Scripture relates how Samuel shared God's word with Saul, advising him that "the Spirit of the LORD will come upon you, and you will prophesy...and be turned into another man" (1 Samuel 10:6, NKJV). We learn that the Spirit descended as a dove upon Jesus as He began His ministry (Matthew 3:16).

13. The Holy Spirit lives in us, and we know that greater He who lives in us than anyone or anything in this world (1 John 4:4). How can we say that? Scripture teaches us that God is omniscient and omnipresent; that is, He knows all and is everywhere (Proverbs 15:3; Psalms 139:1-18; Ephesians 1:9-11).

14. He will fight for us (Exodus 14:13-14; Nehemiah 4:20).

Chapter 7 -Lyrics of Generation Z Arising (YouTube) Spoken Word by Matthew McCluskey

Chapter 8- After Thought

1. However, as the Apostle Paul wrote to the Roman church, "[s] hall we continue to sin that grace may abound? Certainly not (Romans 6:1-2, NKJV)!" We can't flippantly take advantage of God's grace and mercy in that way - by knowingly sinning and being hard-hearted and expecting Him to just accept our sin and us. God doesn't want us to be like the world; He wants us to be transformed truly into His children who demonstrate His perfect will to the world (Romans 12:2).

2. (1 Peter 3:12). We know that whatever we ask for in prayer and in belief, we will receive (Mark 11:24)

3. Jesus told those who followed Him that He would do whatever they asked in His Name so that the Father would be glorified through Him—the Son (John 14:13). John assures us that we can have confidence in approaching God because, if we ask anything according His will, He hears us and, because He hears us, He will grant our petitions (1 John 5:14-15).

4. When we take these actions, then He will hear from heaven, forgive, and heal our land (2 Chronicles 7:14).

5. At God's direction, He prayed earnestly that it would not rain, and no rain fell on the land for three and a half years. Yet, when God led, he prayed again, the rain came, and fruitfulness was restored to the land (James 5:17-18).

6. Because salvation for all certainly is God's will (John 3:16; 2 Peter 3:9).

7. Paul and the disciples devoted themselves to prayer, asking the Lord to open hearts the gospel message, and we see the number of believers increasing exponentially (Acts 16:5, 13-15).

8. Jesus said that we are to love one another, just as He has loved us and that this type of love would be what marked us as His disciples to an onlooking world (John 13:34-35).

9. If anyone boasts, "I love God," and goes right on hating his brother or sister, thinking nothing of it, he is a liar. If he won't love the person he can see, how can he love the God he can't see? The command we have from Christ is blunt: Loving God includes loving people. You've got to love both. (1 John 4:20, MSG)

10. Jesus loved all people - all races, all backgrounds, all economic statuses. If we truly have accepted Christ as Savior, He has implanted His Holy Spirit in us, which means that we have that same capacity to love (1 John 4:16).

11. If I speak with human eloquence and angelic ecstasy but don't love, I'm nothing but the creaking of a rusty gate. If I speak God's Word with power, revealing all [H]is mysteries and making everything plain as day, and if I have faith that says to a mountain, "Jump," and it jumps, but I don't love, I'm nothing. If I give everything I own to the poor and even go to the stake to be burned as a martyr, but I don't love, I've gotten nowhere. So, no matter what I say, what I believe, and what I do, I'm bankrupt without love. (1 Corinthians 13:1-3, MSG)

Reading Sources

David Wilkerson. *God's Hidden Remnant*

Dr. Ray Pritchard. *The Great Commission, Does It Matter.* Christianity Today

Fuchsia Pickett. *A Divine Revelation of the Coming Revival: The Next Move of God.*

Kenneth Hagin. *Triumphant Church, Dominion and Power Over Darkness*

Andrew Chalmers. *God is Raising Up an Army-Take the City*

Debbie Przbybyiski. *The Power of a Praying Church;* Intercessors Arise

Tisha Shedd. *Difference Between Spiritual Warfare*

Pastor Stephen Kyeym. *The New Generation of Worshippers in the 21st Century*

Mario Murillo. *Vessels of Fire and Glory*

Enoch Anti. *Emergence of a New Generation: Behold I do a New Thing*

John Piper. *Every Race it Reign and Worship-Desiring God*, January 1998-, Race & Ethnic Harmony

John Piper. *I'm the Light of the World- Desiring God*

David Platt. *Something Needs to Change- A Call to Make Your Life Count in a World of Urgent Need*

Robert Henderson. *Father, Friend and Judge.*

Jeremiah Johnson. Judgement on the House of God- Cleansing and Glory

David Legs. *God's New Thing -Preach the Word*

David Wilkerson. *God is Doing a New Thing*, YouTube

Author Card

Books and Publications

Women of Faith Living Your Dreams- Accepting the Call to Leadership- Leading Where You Are

Made in God's Image to Live for His Glory: Embracing Your Creative Purpose

The Better than Abundant Life: Doing Life God's Way

Still Slaves in America: Working Together to Break the Chains of Poverty

Broken and Divided: America and the Church- Waiting for the God's Kingdom to be Unveiled

Change Your Life- Change Your Words

CPSIA information can be obtained
at www.ICGtesting.com
Printed in the USA
FSHW020435240421
80653FS